MW00848519

Raising J. Holiday

A Mother's Untold Story

Frances Wellington

April Rain Publications

AU, CAN, FR, DE, IT, IN, JP, UK, US

April Rain Publications

Raising J. Holiday, A Mother's Untold Story

© Copyright 2013 by Frances Wellington
Cover Design: A.A. Marquette

ISBN 9781615395767

Printed in the United States of America

Library of Congress Catalog Card No.: On File

ACKNOWLEDGEMENTS

First I would like to thank *The King of Kings* who died on the cross for me, and who is the head of my life. He is my best friend and will be until eternity. I must thank my mother—a.k.a. Mudd whom I call my million dollar mom. Thank you for just being there for me all my life. She always told me, "Frances, remember, whatever you want in life—no matter what people tell you, you're just as good as anyone else." As a result, I am a woman who perseveres in all that I put my hands and my mind to. I'd like to thank my six biological sisters for always standing with me throughout my life. We are just like trees; when one branch hurts the others feel the pain.

I am giving my son and daughters a standing ovation for being there for me when things in my life went sour. My son made sure I had a house to call my own and my daughters were just as supportive. I love my grandkids, they are the greatest. They always made me smile when I didn't feel like it. When my grandson Diego was around, missing my son was less painful. I thank Pastor Hyman and her congregation for all their encouragement. Hilda Garcia, thank you for interceding for me when I didn't have the strength to pray for myself.

I can't end these acknowledgements without thanking all of my friends, especially the ones that have been true to me down through the years. I must thank two special women too. They have been my friends since this poor little country girl sat her feet on Virginia soil…thank you Shirley Avery and Deborah Harris. To Diane Gray, I'm grateful for all your advice, and for the many things you've told me which have come to pass.

Dr. Philip MacCarthy, my friend, I'm grateful for both your medical and legal advice. My brother Chester, I'm thankful for your laughter, always. I thank Kitty and her three sons for their friendship.

I want to thank Justin Winthers and Corey Green because you guys were instrumental in helping my son to find his musical path; I am forever grateful. I would also like to personally thank April A. Marquette, if not for her expertise, I would not have published this book at this time. You're a Godsend, the greatest. To everyone else, if you think I missed you, I didn't. You were just in the thank you for all my friends.

I want to thank all of my son's bodyguards, past and present; just to name a few — Gregg a.k.a. Slow, Big Wes, and Mase. Thank you for traveling the world with my son as you protect him.

DEDICATION

For my late husband Butch,

It's been 19 years since I've seen your handsome face and heard your voice. Oh how I wish you were here with me, to share in our son's success. Nevertheless, I'm proud to have raised such a wonderful man, one with great strength and honor. Even though you are not here, I still feel your presence around me. Thanks again for the gift you left me—our son. The quality time you spent with us is more precious now than then. Butch, I remember when you looked at me and said "The Best was yet to come." You were not wrong, and I am often reminded of this.

CONTENTS

CONTENTS

PREFACE

It was October 1998, a few days before Halloween. The leaves were turning colors and falling from the trees. The season was changing, like always. In the universe nothing ever remains static. I knew this from experience. As I left work I had an eerie sense of foreboding, a knot in my stomach like something wasn't quite right, like something dramatic was about to happen. When I arrived home I didn't park in front of the house as I normally did. Instead I felt urgency, almost a sixth sense to park in the rear of the complex.

Inside the house my son Nahum and my stepson were in the upstairs bedroom. They were talking the way they normally did, but something seemed different.

 "What's going on boys?" I asked expecting a quick response as I stopped a moment, before passing the room.

"Nothing Ma, just talking about girls," they said almost too quickly.

That wasn't it, but I wouldn't find out the real truth until minutes later. I went downstairs and took an empty cola bottle off the table. Instead of throwing it away in the house, I went outside and threw it in the trash.

As I turned around to walk inside the house, nearly sixty boys had gathered in the front of my building. I immediately recognized them as a part of a street gang that made trouble and spray painted their name and gang sign all over the neighborhood.

I instantly understood what I had been nervously anticipating all day. They had come for my son. I knew he had been having trouble at school with some of the young men. He was a handsome fellow and more than a few of the girls liked him. He'd also been singing at the school talent shows. Before that night I never would have believed that petty childhood jealousies could erupt into a gangland mob like the one that was spinning out of control about five feet from my front door.

Apparently Nahum and my stepson had heard the boys coming and came outside to face them head on. Bravery overtook reason. Although my son was a good fighter, there was no way he and his step-brother could fight sixty boys alone.

There were two leaders who stood in front egging the group on. Tee was a tall boy whose accent placed him from Africa or some Caribbean country. Jay was a little light-skinned boy with a big afro.

I tried to urge my two boys back inside the house but they refused. They weren't going to be known as punks at school or in the neighborhood.

"Boys, go inside," I commanded. They didn't move. They stood flat-footed, facing the two leaders of the group. Nahum had always been an obedient child, even after his father died. He had never given me an ounce of trouble and followed instructions. But that day was different. He just wasn't going to be a coward, even if it meant being disobedient.

I recognized Tee; he'd been the boy that had dropped Nahum off at home a few days before.

"Young man, what's your name?" I asked.

"John," he defiantly responded.

"Your name ain't no damn John," Nahum knowingly revealed .

"Listen," I said loudly, to make sure the entire gang heard me. "If you boys don't leave the front of my house, I'm calling 911."

The boys surged forward, strengthened by the cowardice of a mob mentality.

"Listen, John or whatever your name is," I said, "my son will fight you one-on-one, and I promise he'll beat you all over this complex." I went on to boldly state, "But you are not going to gang up on him today. Not today, not any day."

I looked at the yard as I was talking to the young men and trying to get my boys inside the house. Then my stepson ran into the house. A few seconds passed, and from behind my back I heard *CLICK-UP*. When I turned around, there stood my stepson holding my husband's shotgun. The crowd of boys edged backward.

"Now what, niggas?" he asked while pointing the gun into the crowd.

For a moment I was inert with shock. In my mind I could see dead boys all over the yard, their blood splattered on the ground. I couldn't let that happen.

"Give me the gun," I demanded, while I repeated the first verse of Psalm 91.

"No ma, no. They trying to kill us," he pled.

"Give...me...that gun," I demanded again. When he didn't give it to me, I snatched it out of his hand with my right hand and pushed Nahum, my son in the house with my left.

Inside the house Nahum punched a hole in the wall. His anger flared up in his face and his voice.

I had never seen him so angry.

"Ma let me go back out there. They're disrespecting you! Sorry sons of b - - - - - s. It takes 60 for two?"

I held the gun with one hand and called 911 with the other . I was shaking, but I held the gun and paced back and forth in my living room. This was not the life I wanted for my son. This was not his destiny, to be surrounded and attacked by evil and destroyed...

The police didn't bother to show up—but why would they? In their minds it was just another case of some black boys trying to kill another black boy.

Still, I will never forget the day God saved my son's life, so that he could become . . . *J. Holiday*.

~ WHAT MY MOTHER MEANS TO ME ~

Nahum G

On the day of my birth my mother and I made a special pact.

I love her and she loves me, I know that to be a fact.

Sometimes we argue and fuss, but I know I'm in the wrong.

One day in my life I want to write this special person a song.

She's always been a special person, but once second on my list.

If only I could bring my father back with just one wish.

When my father first left my life, at the tender age of eleven

I thought about him every day,

hoping his soul had flown to heaven.

As I look into the future, present, and past,

I know who my special person is . . . first, second, and last.

Raising J. Holiday, A Mother's Untold Story

1 / THE SHARECROPPER'S DAUGHTER

It was a dark and cold night in the winter of 1953, with no rustling of leaves, no full moon, and no cars passing by. Our family lived in the country—the boondocks really—seemingly far away from everything and everybody else in the world. There was no inside toilet; if those even existed we couldn't afford to have one. Yet my mom felt the urgency to use the bathroom. Not long before this she'd said to my dad, "Luke, you'd better go get the doctor because I feel this baby is coming, soon."

My mom already had three small children, so I would be number four, or maybe I should say I almost *wasn't* number four. I say that because although she already had three children, with me, she didn't realize she was in labor. But she'd had labor pains before, when she'd had my older siblings… Anyway, my mom went to the outside toilet by herself, because my sisters and brother were asleep, and they were too young anyway to be of much help.

Back inside the little country house, feeling me coming, she laid on the bed. Since the midwife wasn't there yet my mom pulled me out—and stretched my neck. That is why my neck is long. So there I was, born before my father and the doctor returned, not only into a segregated world, but also into a life of poverty.

It wasn't all bad though, but then again, things weren't all good either. My parents were sharecroppers, and as their children, as soon as we came of age so were we. Although ours was a life of poverty, my parents did the best they could to provide, and they didn't have just one child, but eleven. Still, my mom was a praying woman who always encouraged her children. She told us we were just as good as other people, and she made us feel we could do anything.

For that reason, even though we could wind up absent from school for weeks, or sometimes months at a time, we would catch up with the other kids whenever we returned to class. We were often out because we had to work in the field; it didn't matter the season. We had no choice because my dad was always borrowing money from his boss. In turn we had to work off that debt.

Thank God we were smart kids because no matter how long we would stay out of school I would get A's and B's like I had been there the entire year. As I got older, I wanted to be involved in any school activity that I could. In a way, I was trying to escape our home life, for many reasons, one of which was my father was an alcoholic...

A lot of my young life was lived during the time of segregation when many things happened. They are things that I will share with you in another book. Right now, I really want to tell you about things that happened *later* in my life, after my son was born. But I didn't want to jump right in without introducing myself. I wanted to tell you a little about me, like where I came from and things like that.

So now that you know a bit, let's begin...

2 / BUTCH

It was fall 1979 when Butch came into the picture. You see, I had to put my 1978 Gremlin in the shop. At the time I was attending beauty school near a mechanic's place and one day before I headed to school, I stopped by. I needed to see if there was anything that auto mechanic shop could do to help my raggedy car.

A young man told me that the person that could really help me had been out for a few weeks. But, the youngster said, the particular man that he'd spoken of was due back in a few days. I said, "I hope this is the best mechanic you have on staff." The young man assured me that the staff person that I would see was the best in the shop. So I left my car there, but I kept checking day after day, waiting for this magic man to show up.

Finally, one day I walked in and a gentleman asked if he could help me. I said. "Yes, I am looking for the best mechanic to show up for work—and as long as I've been waiting for him, I expect him to do a superb job on my car." The man smiled and said his name was Butch. He also said *he* was the mechanic that I had been waiting for.

Unperturbed, I said, "Pleased to meet you Butch. My name is Frances, and I hope you can fix my car." Butch told me he would start on it that day. I let him know there was no hurry because I needed him to keep it there until I got the money to get it out. I also said I needed front and back brakes, and Butch said he would take care of it. Before I left, I made sure he knew not to do anything until he let me know what it would cost.

Well, that mechanic gave me an estimate, and I told him to fix things. Trying to finish beauty school, I did not have a lot of money, so when Butch called and told me to let him know when I could pick up my car, I said I'd let him know. Many days went by. These were days where I would pass that shop while on my way to and from lunch. I would see the mechanic who'd worked on my car rolling my windows up or down, and starting my car so the battery wouldn't die. I have to tell you. Although I didn't see that man taking care of anybody else's car like that, I was thankful.

One day, on foot, I left beauty school. I was on my way to the bus stop. Out driving, Butch stopped to see if I wanted a ride. I told him no and walked on, but he kept sitting in his car beside me, bothering me, so finally I gave in. As he drove me home, he started to talk about his life and his job as a mechanic. He also told me
the reason he'd been off from work for so long. He had burnt his arm opening up a hot radiator cap. He then said for me not to try it. Why was he telling me that? I wondered. I wasn't his wife or anything. In truth, I barely knew him.

Butch also told me where his family lived…in Maryland. He said he was divorced and had a young son. He admitted that he thought his marriage hadn't worked out because both he and his former wife had been young. Butch then wanted to know more about me.

I told him I had two small daughters and that I lived with my sisters. I admitted I was going to beauty school so that I could take care of my girls. I said I was going to get my cosmetology license because I was determined not to be a welfare recipient.

Butch told me where he lived, with a cousin. He also said he wanted to get to know me better. I told him I was in the church—real heavy—and trying to live right. That didn't scare him off though.

He began talking about the bible. He had a lot of knowledge, but he had no idea where Jesus fit in the puzzle. He admitted that he had asked God to send him someone who could help him. But he'd told God not to send him a man.

"Well," I said, "Jesus answered your prayer."

Butch wanted to continue to take me home until I got the money to get my car out of the shop. One day before I got my car back, he was driving me and all of a sudden he said, "I think I will ask to marry you."

I said, "I don't think so. You don't know me, and I don't know you."

I forgot to tell you that a few weeks earlier my sister had informed me that God would bless me with a mate. I didn't pay her much attention. I didn't even tell anybody that although Butch and I had recently met, just weeks prior, I still felt a connection with him. I did tell him though that I would tell my parents about him wanting to marry me. I said, "You tell yours too, and we will see what they think."

Well my mom was okay; she just wanted to meet him and get to know him better. But Butch didn't get the same reaction. His dad was okay with things, but his mom was tripping— because I had two kids.

Added to that drama was my oldest daughter who was almost seven years old. When I told her, she wasn't pleased. My youngest daughter was almost two, so she didn't know the difference one way or another. When I told my sister about everything, all she said about Butch was, "Just make sure he will be a good father to your kids, and a good husband." Then my sisters started planning my wedding, which was in one month's time.

Despite the short amount of time in which to prepare, the wedding turned out to be superb. But before my wedding took place, I got a call from an old boyfriend, whose only intent was to get on my nerves.

Why was he calling, out of the blue, aggravating me? I wondered, and went for a ride by myself. I did so to clear my head and wound up getting lost, in Georgetown. Back then we had no cell phones, so I pulled my little raggedy car up beside a pay phone. I put the change in and called Butch who told me to stay where I was. Instead of him just giving me directions to get out, he said he would come get me.

When he arrived, I followed his car back to his apartment. I called my sister at home and asked how my girls were. I told her where I was. Then I wound up falling asleep on Butch's couch. We did nothing. I have to say so because people's minds race, and I know you're wondering. When I woke up, I realized he had been sitting there watching me sleep. I'd dozed off because I had been so tired, going to beauty school, taking care of my girls, and working at night at a baby plant where I packed pictures of other people's babies so that I could take care of my own.

As I was getting off his couch, Butch said, "Frances, I fixed you breakfast." While I was still trying to wrap my mind around the fact that I had allowed myself to fall asleep, away from my own home, he brought the breakfast that he had fixed and placed it before me on the coffee table. I thought that was so sweet. I knew right then he was a Godsend, for me. He was a man of integrity.

Our wedding took place a week later. On the day, it was pouring down rain—not a good omen, some would say. My father was supposed to give me away too, but five minutes before my wedding he was still on the beltway! So my soon to be father-in-law had to stand in. Then on the way up the steps, my gown got caught in my shoe. I don't know to this day how I got it out, but I did.

Butch's mom was still upset, with her lips poked out, even on the day of our wedding, but I didn't care and neither did Butch; he wasn't marrying her. All my sisters and brothers, and my mom were in the wedding. One of my sisters sang Stevie Wonder's *For Once in My Life*. I'd asked her to, because that was how I felt; that song described my feelings exactly. My oldest daughter was the flower girl, what choice did she have, whether she liked Butch or not?

It turned out to be a nice day after all. The only thing was… my pastor was very old, so I couldn't really understand what she was saying until she got to 'I pronounce you man and wife,' and 'kiss the bride.'

That was the happiest day of my life because I was marrying the man of my dreams. I knew he would be a good husband and father. Sure, my two daughters weren't his, but he never looked at them as step-kids.

After the reception was over, we went on an overnight honeymoon in The District. When we got to the place, I sat down on a chair and told my husband that unless he promised to take me to see my mom later, I wasn't going to take off my gown and do anything with him. Poor Butch, he said he would take me to see my mom. I was real close to her, and it wasn't like I was single anymore and could just go over any time I felt like it. I had a husband and a new life. A lot of things were going to change for us.

Butch and I started our new life in Virginia and we loved each other so very much. The first six months were the greatest. You'd have thought I was in a royal palace. Butch used to even sing the song *I'll Never Love This Way Again* by Dionne Warwick while bringing me breakfast in bed.

By the way, I met him just before my oldest daughter's birthday, and we were married in less than two months. I don't know if at the time whether Butch knew how profound him saying that he would never love this way again was, but he was right, and we had wonderful years together.

Butch said he was very happy to be married to me and that he had finally found someone to spend the rest of his life with, someone with whom he could share all of his dreams.

Raising J. Holiday, A Mother's Untold Story

3 / INTRODUCING MY SON

As I think back on my life, I realize more and more that at an age that I certainly hadn't planned, I became a mom. Anyway, I had a daughter first, and then another. Both of those pregnancies were very easy, and almost a well-kept secret. Unless you knew me personally, you would never have known that I was with child either time. The girls were very quiet the full nine months, *but* it was *not* that way with my son.

My husband had talked to me on several occasions, saying he wanted to have another son to raise and love. You see, he already had one from a previous relationship. I can't say exactly how I knew, but when I conceived, I knew that would be my last child. I would also later find out that my husband knew his time in this world was short. Yet other than God, nobody else—not even I had the slightest idea.

When I conceived however, I asked God to please let me have a son. Listen to me. When you ask God for something be careful. Think it through too, before the final seal is placed because often you will get just what you asked for. So at the time, I was working at a big named hair cutting place, doing about nineteen to twenty heads per day in an eight hour span. Many times I'd be right in the middle of a haircut, and I would have to stop and go down the hall to the restroom, or I had to simply sit my fat self down, because boy was I heavy! I was waddling when I walked. It was terrible.

During that pregnancy, I knew I was carrying a boy because he kicked my butt the entire nine months—it just didn't make any sense. Well, I guess since his sisters hardly kicked at all, he was making up for them. While carrying my middle child Yolanda, she couldn't move around after about seven months, because she was just too long, and my oldest daughter Quineice had plenty of room because she'd been shorter.

With my son however, a lot of the time I thought there was another baby inside with him, because it seemed like he was always fighting; getting on my nerves. He reminded me of the bible's Jacob and Esau, fighting inside their mother's womb, but my son was fighting all by himself.

When he was born in the fall of 1981, I remember...it was kind of cool that morning. My water broke at about five a.m. Two of my sisters had stayed the night with me so my husband could get a break. Casually, I walked into the room where they were sleeping and told them what happened. I said I need to go to the hospital. I wasn't nervous, but they were. They acted like *they* were having the baby. I never could figure that out.

The rescue squad arrived to take me to the hospital, but first they wanted to ask me questions, to make sure I was alert. Come to find out later, it wasn't me who needed to be alert, it was them.

The ride to the hospital was kind of bumpy and when we arrived, the rescue people told admissions when they rolled me passed the desk that I was white and blond. Thus, the admissions staff were looking everywhere for the blond white lady. When I got tired of all the running back and forth I asked, "Are y'all looking for me?"

The admissions staff asked, "Were you just brought in by the rescue squad?" My reply was, "Yes." Then the staff said of the rescue squad, "This doesn't make any sense for them not to get this right, because she—" meaning me, "—is nowhere close to blond, and she's certainly not white." Also speaking of the rescue squad, the staff said, "They need to go home and get some rest." I was lying there smiling the whole time.

I don't remember whether or not my sisters came with me, but I was glad that I was finally giving birth to my son. That didn't stop me from being upset with my husband though, because I'd told him to go out, but not stay all night.

I was in a lot of pain, but I didn't want any meds. I wanted to have a natural birth. The doctor asked if I was sure I didn't want meds. I told her yes, and asked if she'd seen my husband.

About an hour before I gave birth, he came strolling in, like he was the cat's meow. He asked did I have the baby yet and put his hand on my stomach. He was teasing, maybe, but I was so angry with him. I told him to leave me alone, and that he was too late. By then, the pain was worse than ever, so I wanted meds, but for me it was too late. By the time the hospital staff moved me from the labor table to the delivery table, a bald headed boy came rolling out, yelling to the top of his lungs. I should have known then that he would be a singer.

When I saw him and he didn't have any hair, I figured he would be a thinker. I felt like the hard part was over, and the doctors cleaned him up and gave him to me. I had delivered

 a six pound, four ounce, eighteen inch-long baby boy. For some reason, while looking at him, I figured if he was anything like he had been in my womb, I was going to have my hands full.

I was yet a little angry with Butch for not being there in the beginning, but previously I'd promised that he could name our baby. So my husband tells me he wants to name our baby boy Nahum Thornton. I looked at that man like he was crazy. I told him I was not naming my son that. I didn't like the 'Thornton' part. To me it threw everything off. I'm almost sure I pointed at Butch when I said I had a Quineice and a Yolanda, and the new name didn't sound right.

When the nurse brought the birth certificate, I said I didn't have a name yet. So my son went twenty-four hours without a name.

I really don't know why I was tripping because Nahum is a minor prophet in the bible, and I am an Ordained Minister for God's sake. I think I could have dealt with the Nahum, but Thornton—which was my husband's father's middle name—was smack in the middle. I didn't care whose name it was; to me it didn't make any kind of sense.

Well, after twenty four hours, I finally gave in. Taking our bald headed baby home, we started to enjoy our son.

Raising him was a pleasure. He was quiet and very calm. Nahum was truly a fast learner, reminding me of a saying that the old folks had about smart babies. They often said they were most likely getting out of the way for the next baby, which was the least of my worries.

My husband didn't believe in pacifiers, but I wanted to give Nahum a pacifier, once in a while, if he was sleepy, but no, my husband was against it. One night though, I left the baby with his dad and he was crying for me so hard that my husband took the top of one the baby bottles and put some tissue in it so that our son could be quiet. After that, my husband couldn't get a pacifier fast enough!

While potty training, I used to stand my small son next to his dad so that he could watch what his dad was doing, and it worked! Nahum was potty trained and walking at about a year old.

When he was three years old, I was still working for the hair cutting chain. Every day my son and I walked to the bus stop where we caught the big coach that would take us to his school. Once there, I would walk him inside the building. I made sure he was okay; then I'd leave and walk to my job.

Now one day, during my break I had to pick my son up from school and take him back to the shop with me. He was just sitting there real quiet, while I finished a perm. Coming out of the back, the manager asked whose child he was. I looked boldly at her and said, "Mine, who wants to know?"

The manager shot back, "You know you can't have your child in here while you work, so you have to take him home and come back and finish that perm."

First of all, she didn't know who she was dealing with because when it comes to my kids, I was not—and still am not—to be played with. So I looked Manger right in the face and told her that if I took my son all that long way home, I would not be back. I didn't say it but I'm telling you; if I'd had to ride the bus all the way home, once I got there, I would have had no baby sitter. Therefore, I said to Manager, "I tell you what… You can take this job and ram it. *You* finish the perm." I quit that day. I got my stuff, took my son's little hand, and walked to the bus stop.

In the course of time, I got a job as a cosmetology teacher. What's more, my son went to school in the same building, on the same floor, right across the hall! Talk about God blessing me! I had lunch with him every day. I did, so that my boy who was growing up fast could see my face.

A few years later, look how God blessed me again. I got a job in *management* with that same hair cutting chain—the one I'd left due to that stupid stuff with my then-manager, but now I was in a different location.

I have to tell you the reason why I had quit. I knew I could do hair at home and make just as much money. I had done it before. Prior to me getting that job, I had been doing hair. I was a beautician on wheels—so don't play with me! And I'll tell you something else. While my kids were growing up I always told them, "Don't ever leave a job unless you have another one waiting for you."

At church, I happened to be one of the lead soloists in the choir. I also sang with my sisters. We had a singing group. At our church I directed the little kids' choir which my son was in. One of my girls was in it too. I think I put my son in the choir, and he enjoyed being with the other kids. At the time, I wasn't aware that he was a singer in the making. Sometime later, he also started playing the drums, and the piano, and he was good. I'm not just saying that because I'm his mother.

But back to my kids…they were so well-mannered until people used to believe I beat them. I didn't have to. You just

have to know how to be a good mom, and not just in name only. All I had to do was look at my children and that was enough. If you don't believe me, you can ask each one and they will tell you.

Now dealing with my son's name situation, nobody could pronounce it, no one other than the family. Nahum, my son even had a babysitter who called him 'Lab,' like he was a science project or something.

Other people called him Neum. My poor son got so tired of people not knowing how to pronounce his name until all through his early years he didn't like his name. He often said when he got older he would change it. Believe me, he did just that.

One day he came home from school and told me his name wasn't Nahum anymore. I asked, "What is it now?" He said one of his cousins had started calling him Nate. I just laughed, because my son was happy with his new nickname. He still didn't like it when adults butchered his name, but I told him, "It doesn't matter to me whether you like things or not, you nor your sisters will disrespect anybody, about any-thing—because if I hear about it, I will beat your butt." My kids knew that whatever I said, I would do.

During her senior year in high school, my oldest daughter got involved with a drug dealer. I knew that beady-eyed young man was not right when I saw him looking under-eyed at me. I told my daughter to leave that character alone. My son didn't even like him.

Some people used to think my son was a momma's boy, but that wasn't it, at all. He just stayed real close to me. Come to find out, he called himself being the man of the house—but he didn't pay one bill! I looked out for my girls the same way, but the only thing was, my boy was the youngest. He was eleven when his dad passed away, and I was determined not to lose him to drugs or the streets.

After my husband's death, I was in no shape to do much of anything. I was just frozen in time. I was more devastated than anybody really knew. I told God I didn't know how I would make it, but, I promised, I was *not* going to lose my son to life's evils. At that time, my oldest daughter was twenty one, and my middle daughter was fifteen, so I had a lot on my plate. I had to quickly come out of my trance, because if anyone needed me it was my son, because he'd loved his dad and they had been close.

The week that my husband passed away, he and my son had done many things together. Therefore, for Butch to just die like that was more than my son could handle.

I was glad that Nahum had been chosen to go to James Madison University for three weeks to be mentored by big brothers. That was the best thing that could have happened to him. He left a very reserved boy, but he returned home a leader. He had also joined a step team while he was away, and has loved stepping ever since—and can he step! I was so happy to see my son come out of his shell. It was a lot, dealing with his father's death, yet slowly but surely my son began to do better. I'll tell you more in a little while...

I must say, I had so many good times with my kids while they were growing up. We went skating, shopping, and bowling; we had cookouts, and lots of other things. Parents, never forget this, you have to enjoy your kids while they are small. They will grow up before you know it. Then you may wonder where the time went, so quickly.

At the end of every summer I always took my kids school shopping. I told them, "Stick with me and don't be running around." I said, "If I have to stop shopping, then there will be a problem."

Once we were in a store where I was trying my best to find good bargains, but that particular day Nahum kept running under a round rack of clothing. I told him to stop before he hurt himself. He was having a ball, and was not properly listening to me. I told him, "If you hurt your head, I will stop and pray for you and put some Vaseline on your head." I said that would be all I could do.

I've always kept Vaseline and anointing oil in my purse because I never know when I'm going to need it. I also made sure my son knew, "I don't have any money to take you to the hospital." Nahum kept playing and laughing, and in a while I heard him yelling and screaming. I wound up doing just what I'd said. I wiped the trickle of blood off his head, I prayed for him, applied Vaseline, and kept on shopping.

The bible's first command with promise is *honor your mother and father that your days may be long upon the earth.* My kids know I will quote a scripture in a hot minute because I am not ashamed of the gospel. My daughter Yolanda would always say, "Mom, not today…" Her older sister Quineice wasn't quite as bold. Both of them are yet the same way to this day.

When Nahum was six years old, he had to write a journal, and his sisters were helping him spell the words. In his journal, he was attempting to write that he was going to 'hump Carrie this Christmas,'—what kind of foolishness?

But the kids told him that hump was spelled with an e on the end. I told him hump is spelled *without* an e, "And if you have a spelling test Friday," I said, "and hump is on that test and you spell it wrong, I will beat your butt." Well guess what? He had a spelling test and hump was on it, and he spelled it right! I didn't know why the first girl he wanted to hump was Latina—what was that about?

Not knowing it was just before my husband Butch's death, I purchased a beauty salon. I hired all three of my kids to work for me. I always paid them on Saturday, like I did everybody else. The girls followed the rules, but for some reason, Nahum thought just because he was the youngest, he could get away with more than his sisters. Well sometimes that was true, but I knew I had to be strong and not give in.

Now one Saturday we were real busy and Nahum was the janitor. It was his job to keep the hair swept up at all times, but this day he wanted to go play videos with some kids who were waiting for their mom. I told my son that if he left, I would not pay him for the day. Then I let him make his own decision.

He did, and when he got his money he was a day short. It hurt me to my heart to do it, but at the time I had to remain firm so that my son would know that in life he would not always be able do whatever he wanted with no consequences. I believe that's why he is the man that he is today.

Parents, you have to prepare your kids for the real world whether it hurts or not. Hopefully, they will thank you later.

4 / STRANGE HAPPENINGS

My husband Butch was a very laid-back, quiet man, so he wasn't interested in being up front in anything. He didn't have the need that some people have, to always be seen or heard. Since he already knew his time was running out, when the opportunity came for him to dress up, he jumped at the chance, so that I would have lasting memories of him.

Now I don't believe what I'm about to tell you was a coincidence. I feel it was planned by God. At the last minute I was asked to be in my girlfriend's wedding. The dress I was supposed to wear wasn't sized for me, but when I got the call, I told my girlfriend that I would be her bridesmaid. I asked my husband if he would be my escort, and immediately he said he would. He went out and spent his hard earned money and rented a tux. I should have suspected something then, because Butch rarely dressed up, but I'm glad he did for that occasion because to this day I still have a picture of him his tuxedo.

At the time, Butch was giving me a profound message, but I had no idea because he had always promised that he would live to be one hundred and twenty five. Although I knew it was possible because there are many people that have lived well past a hundred years, I just looked at things like this. Butch was promising me that we would grow old together.

Now I know…back then *he knew* we wouldn't… Still, I want to believe that he jumped at the chance for us to take pictures and spend a nice time together so that I would have treasured memories of him—which I do have.

I remember one night I was lying in my bed, I got the unction to go downstairs and pray for my husband. When I got down there, I saw that he'd fallen asleep on his favorite chair, but I went over anyway and prayed for him. Then I went back to bed.

The next day, my girlfriend called to tell me that God was about to put my husband in his rightful place. I got all excited, because I was thinking Butch was about to join me in ministry, but later that week I would find out it wasn't that, after all.

There had been another day, a Thursday when I had been frying chicken. Butch had come home from work, but before he got there I had run out of vegetable oil. That meant I was frying the chicken in Crisco oil. For some unknown reason, laid-back Butch went off! He let me know he wasn't going to eat that chicken. Then the next thing I knew, he was holding his chest and leaning over the kitchen sink.

Concerned, I asked him what was wrong.

Passing it off, he claimed, "Oh it's just gas, nothing to worry about." However, in my gut I knew it was more than that. I suggested taking Butch to the hospital, but he declined.

Then on Friday, he told me that he'd had a dream about my best friend and he wanted to talk to her. My husband also wanted to talk to our eldest daughter, because he wanted to know what he had done to her to make her dislike him. Then last but not least, he wanted me to cut his hair and trim his beard.

I pointed out that it was late and I was tired. Being easy-going, Butch let me off the hook by agreeing that it was late. He said "I forgot, you can't see well late at night." He was teasing, but it was the truth.

5 / FACE TO FACE WITH MY HUSBAND'S CORPSE

Starting out, May 22, 1993 seemed like a normal day, until I fully woke and realized my husband wasn't in bed with me. It was early, on a Saturday morning and although I didn't know it at the time, that was a day that would end in tragedy for me and my children. Yet when I realized my husband wasn't next to me, I went downstairs, where Butch sometimes fell asleep.

When I got to the bottom of the stairs, I peeped around the corner. There he was, in his normal spot, with the big bamboo pillow that he liked to sleep on beneath him. Moving quietly, I just felt like there was something different about that morning, but I hadn't yet figured out what it was. Still, I walked slowly over to where Butch was sleeping and gently touched him. I asked if he was going to work.

He said yes and asked what time it was. I announced it was 7:30 a.m. Butch said that was good because the Post Garage, the auto mechanic shop where he was employed didn't open until 8:00. He said he would be up in a few minutes to shower and prepare for work. I went back upstairs and started to ready myself for the day. I had a big promotion for my salon taking place.

I remember sitting on the side of the bed and talking to God. I felt so strange. I can't explain it, but with reference to my life I had to ask God, "Why did you take me this route?"

God's reply was *I had to take you this way because any other way would have been too easy for you—because you persevere.* Looking back, in hindsight, I realize God knew I wouldn't give up. He knew I would get through even the hardest of things.

By that time I was in the bathroom mirror fixing my hair because I had to look nice. So while I was putting on my makeup, my husband came upstairs to take his shower. While he was drying off, I asked him to drive past the promotion when he finished at the Post Garage. I reminded him that he was a partner in the business and that I wanted him to be with me for the promotion. Butch agreed. He also said he hoped his brother would be there with their mom's car because he wanted to fix her air conditioner.

I remember having a hard time leaving him that morning… because something just didn't seem right. So I kept walking back and forth from the bathroom to the bedroom door, talking to Butch and feeling very restless. It was like I knew something was about to take place. It was just a gut feeling. The last thing I said when I went back to the bathroom was, "Ok Butch, when you finish everything, just come on by the promotion." It was an outside event, near where I would put our small son on the train to Fredericksburg. That day Nahum was going sightseeing with other kids.

I will never forget the look that my son's father gave me. It seemed Butch looked right *through* me, but he wasn't saying a word. I gave him a kiss and bounced on out the door like I usually did. I would later find out…that was to be the last time I saw my husband…*alive*.

I picked up my sister and mom, so they could help me with the promotion for the salon. With my daughter in the car too, I drove to the site. We had been there just long enough to set up. We were out doors with lots of other people who would also promote their businesses, and they too were fixing their booths and tables. I was busy, but in less than fifteen minutes, I heard someone call my name.

I looked up and saw one of my stylists racing across the field toward me. I wondered what she was doing there, because she was supposed to be back at the shop.

"Fran!" she called, out of breath.

I wanted to know what was up, and my stylist said, "Your mother-in-law called. She said your husband has fallen out, on the job—and they can't wake him up!"

At that moment, I started drifting into shock. I also had flashbacks to that morning when I'd been at home and had felt unable to leave; I told you I'd been going back and forth talking to Butch.

The stylist said I needed to go. "Go to the Post Garage." Yes, because Butch had fallen out and they couldn't get him to respond, to anything!

Hurriedly, because something was wrong with Butch, I gave my sister and my mom instructions for watching my table until I returned. I told my daughter, who was having a baby at the time, to stay put. I said I would go and see what was wrong. I got in my car, and I was talking to God. I told him I didn't know what was happening, but whatever it was I needed His help to deal with it.

I drove straight to the post garage, but while doing so, I had a funny feeling that after that day my life was going to change, forever. As I headed to the garage to check on Butch, I started praying out loud, asking God to give me the strength to face whatever I would confront.

I arrived at the garage about fifteen minutes later, and as I was getting out of the car, Mike, who was my husband's supervisor, met me with tears streaming down his face.

He said, "Butch had a heart attack."

Feeling dazed and in shock I asked, "Well, where is he?"

I was told that Butch was at DeWitt Army Hospital.

There is so much that happened that day, until you will have to read about some of it in my next book, the one about my own life. However, I got back in my car and drove right around the corner. That's how close the hospital was. By that time, I was still aware of my surroundings, even though I had slowly started to drift into something like shocked disbelief.

At the hospital, I parked in front of the emergency entrance. Before I could turn off my car and get out, my husband's brother came towards me. Feeling frantic, I asked, "What's happening?"

Brother said, "He's gone."

Shocked and disbelieving, I asked, "Gone where?!"

Then Brother softly said, like it would hurt less, "Frances, he's...*gone.*" And with tears in his eyes, he walked away. Right then and there, I knew that my brother-in-law had told me that my husband was *dead.* I looked up towards heaven and said to God, "If this man is saying what I think he is, You are going to have to give me a second wind, because I am not going to be able to deal with this."

Then I truly felt a second wind, the strength to face all that I needed to. It rose up inside of me. That was when doctors and nurses came running toward me, wanting to know whether or not I was 'The Mrs.' I replied, "Yes, I am she."

They said, "We are so sorry; we couldn't save him." They told me they gave Butch three shock treatments, and still they had been able to get my husband back.

I asked if I could see him. The hospital staff said they needed to clean him up first. "So just take a seat there," they indicated a designated area. They said, "We will come get you in a few minutes."

While I sat, I just stared at the ceiling, wondering whether this news was true or not. I prayed not. Finally, staff members came in to escort me into Emergency where Butch was. I told them to stay back, please; I didn't need them to go in with me. I wanted to spend time with my husband alone.

I went in the little emergency room and there was my man, lying there with his eyes half-open. I said, "Butch, what are you doing here? You were supposed to be helping with the business, and the ministry. You said you wanted to be a race car driver."

I got no reply, so I looked up toward heaven, and asked God was this supposed to be my first resurrection? I wondered if I was supposed to call Butch back from the dead. From God I got no reply. Seeing the change from my husband's pockets, and his keys lying on the little table next to the bed, I walked to his right side. With my heart breaking, I leaned over and kissed him on his forehead and whispered in his ear, "Butch, I love you, take your rest."

At that moment he closed his eyes. Although the doctors had thought he had already been gone, evidently, my husband had been waiting to say farewell *to me*.

As I write this, I'm tearing up. I can hardly see, and my heart is breaking all over again, even though it has been nineteen years since we experienced all this terrible hurtfulness...

When I stepped outside the curtain, doctors and nurses were waiting. They told me, "Go to the break room, have some coffee or tea." They said they had to prepare my husband's things for release. But I couldn't move. I was frozen in place.

While I stood there, I heard the doctors doing things in the room where Butch's body lay. I was sure I heard some type of wrapping up. A few minutes passed, but to me it seemed like a day. Then suddenly the curtains were pulled back, exposing my Butch, wrapped up like the bible's Lazarus, for his burial.

When the gurney passed me with Butch's wrapped body on it, I leaned over in slow motion and cried out, "Butch!" Then I said, "Oh never mind, Butch is gone and he won't be coming back."

His personal belongings were finally released to me, and as I was walking out of the hospital door, Butch's boss was there, speaking. He said, "This is going to take a minute, so you will need to take some time for yourself."

As I approached the exit door, a warm tear streamed down my left cheek. Even though I was in a state of shock, and feeling frozen with grief, I managed to drive back to my promotion. When I was almost there I saw my mom and my oldest daughter coming in my direction. I stopped the car and allowed them to get in. Then my mom wanted to know, "What was wrong with Butch?"

My monotone reply was, "Mom, he's dead."

She grabbed me and we both began to weep. I look over at my daughter and she had such a sad look on her face.

After something as drastic as losing my husband, I still went back to my salon and continued business as usual. I stayed about an hour. I was aware that I yet had to get my small son off the train too because he would soon be returning from his sightseeing trip to Fredericksburg. I knew that my shop workers needed to be paid, and I still had even more things to handle. When I was seated behind my desk, all settled in, the stylists wanted to know, "What happened to Butch?"

I said I would tell them in a few minutes, but I was mightily battling back tears. I continued to make sure everybody paid me for the week, so that in turn I could pay others. I was in such a state of shock and in such a freeze-zone, but no one really noticed. As the stylists began to leave, one by one, they wanted to know if Butch was okay. I think they all were stunned when I said, "Well, Butch is dead..." They began to cry, feeling sorry for me, but I refused to let them see me cry.

I stayed at the shop, to make sure everything was taken care of for the week. I knew I would be gone for at least that long. It was why I asked my best stylist to run the shop for me while I was out; I had to bury my husband.

We did not have cell phones back then and my son Nahum was only eleven so I had to go get him from the train. When he got off, despite the fact that I was still in a functioning state of shock, I asked, "How was your trip?"

He said it was fine and that he'd had a good time. All he wanted to know was if we were going to McDonald's because earlier I'd promised him that we would. I went to the drive-thru to get his food. As I was driving home, he was eating his fries and I was wondering how on earth I was going to tell this little happy boy that his father was dead. My son had such a good time on his trip, then he'd gone to McDonald's, as promised, and now I had to rain on his parade. It was horrible.

At the house, at the table, he finished eating. In my bedroom I was pacing, trying to figure out how to tell my son the news about his father. I told Nahum to come into my bedroom. I said I had something to tell him. Before I told him, I held him. I hugged him because I knew he was going to cry. I spoke softly and said, "Your dad is dead."

Broken-hearted and sobbing, my son began trying to get away from me.

My mother was at the house by then and I called down to her. I asked if she would take Nahum for a walk to calm him down. Our cocker spaniel Crystal was just sitting there, aware that something was wrong.

I called my sister in Georgia and told her. A believer, she said if I felt that some of the promises that God had made to me were violated, then I could go over to the hospital and call my husband's spirit back into his body. Anguished and hurt, I told her that I would sleep on it. I said when I woke up in the morning I would have a confrontation with God.

My mom and my sister—the one who'd gone to the promotion with me—spent the night so that they could help with the kids. The next morning I said I didn't want to be bothered, that I needed to talk to God. I locked my bedroom door and went in my bathroom where I could pray. I was crying so much. With tears of hurt and anger streaming down I began to tell God that I felt that some of the promises I'd received about Butch had been violated.

I was on my knees when I felt a soft breeze come through my bathroom window. then I heard God's audible voice speak calmly to me. The first thing God said was "*You've walked with me, you preached my gospel, you've kept my statues; I have never lied to you, and there was no violation*."

I asked God what did He mean, there was no violation?

God's reply was that *my husband requested to leave*.

Then I asked, "God, do you have to answer every request?"

His reply was "*Had not I answered Butch's request, then there would have been a violation. Don't worry*," God soothed, "*You will see him* [Butch] *in the resurrection, and he will always be with you in the ministry*." God also told me, "*I will raise you above the people, so just do my will and I will keep my promises*."

I tell you, I was so empty when my husband died, until I

didn't think I would ever find anything to fill that terrible void. However I told God that since Butch requested to leave at such an early age, I would like to live out his days.

I have not yet received answer, so we will see. Still, the first thing that helped me to begin feeling a bit of recovery was seeing my first grandchild. The infant was born a month after my husband's death. My daughter's baby brought me so much joy until I didn't have a lot of time to grieve. I only wished Butch had been around to spend time with our first grandchild. But as I think back, I realize it was like he had already known that he hadn't had much longer. I say that because one night while he lived, Butch had been talking to our grand baby, really to my daughter's belly. He told that baby that he or she needed to hurry up and come. That was the last time Butch saw our daughter before his death.

Another thing that brought me joy during that horrendous time was that I began teaching kids with special needs. Being with those children five days a week gave me a different perspective. It gave me purpose too. By that I mean, I was able to see that my own children were blessed; they were all gifted and talented, where my special needs children were different and they needed me in a dissimilar way. One particular family, whose oldest boy liked Michael Jackson, invited me and my children to dinner. This child had no control over his muscles. Well, I took my son's *Moonwalker* video to the house for this boy. It turned out that while I was speaking with his parents, my special needs boy who was always so happy said, "Frances, I need a haircut!"

He did because he and I often talked about my cosmetology work. But that evening at his home I had to tell him I didn't have any scissors. Well he went rolling off in his wheelchair. He came back after having found some paper scissors.

It was so cute, especially the fact that he had all his sisters and brothers lined up to get their hair cut too. My special needs happy boy said, "Frances, I know you can do it!"

My children watched in astonishment as I held that child's head up and cut his hair with those dull little bitty scissors.

I'm telling you, after cutting all that hair—his and his siblings—my thumb was so red and sore, but I loved every minute of it.

Still my wheelchair-bound boy made me sad when he reminded me that school was ending for the summer. Due to that, he wanted to know who was going to take care of him.

He asked me, "Frances, who is going to fix my hair? Who's going to hold my head up? Who will fix my socks?" He asked because I had done those things for him, every day.

6 / THE FUNERAL

It started out a sad, but very quiet day. Everybody around us was preparing to attend the funeral. I heard no children playing, no dogs barking, not even birds singing in the trees. It was a day that I never want to re-live again. I'd hated the thought of riding in a limo, unless I was going to be in Hollywood. Therefore, I had never dreamed that my first limo ride would be to my husband's funeral.

Since it was scheduled to start at 10:00 a.m., the limo arrived to pick up the family at 9:15 a.m. The ride to the service was quiet too. I was watching my children, especially my son. The kids' grandparents, Butch's parents, rode in the car with us, and the looks on their faces told me they were devastated as well. I'm sure my mother was in the car, but I can hardly remember. I sat there, in a daze, feeling frozen. Yet I do remember that the driver was going really slow, missing every green light, something none of us needed when we just wanted the day to be over.

My husband had always told me that when he died, he didn't want to be buried in a suit. If he only knew that I had almost buried him in jeans, like he requested. As for me and the children, we weren't under any rule to wear black, so we all wore light colors.

It seemed to take forever to arrive at the funeral home, but finally we got there. As we prepared to exit the car I was still in a daze, hoping that someone would touch me and say this was just an April fool's joke, but it wasn't April, and it was no joke. It was May and my second worst day.

As we entered the chapel, and the viewing of the body continued, my mind raced back to earlier that week when strange things had happened, leading up to Butch's death. I told you that there had been a night when I'd been lying in bed and felt the need to go downstairs and pray for Butch who had fallen asleep on his favorite chair. I told you that my girlfriend had called and told me that God was going to put my husband in his rightful place, and that I'd felt excited, thinking Butch was going to join me in ministry. I even remembered the night I'd fried chicken even though I'd run out of vegetable oil. That had been the night that Butch had acted so out of character and wound up clutching his chest afterward. I remembered that he'd claimed he had gas and that it was nothing to worry about, even though I had known it was more than that. And I couldn't forget that I'd suggested taking Butch to the hospital, but he had turned me down.

I remembered that he'd said he wanted to speak to my best friend, and that he'd wanted to talk to our eldest daughter, to set things right with her. How could I forget that last but not least, Butch had wanted me to cut his hair and trim his beard—and I'd told him it was late and I was too tired! Good -naturedly he'd agreed by laughingly stating, "I forgot, you can't see late at night," which was the truth.

Seated at my husband's funeral, I remembered… Butch had never gotten the chance to do any of the things he'd requested. He had died that Saturday.

As I sat there in that packed funeral home I couldn't help but wonder, how had I lived with my husband almost fourteen years, and he'd slipped right through my fingers without me ever knowing he was sick? I told myself, your mate is closer to you than anyone other than God and your family. I had eaten, slept with, walked with, talked with, went shopping with, and prayed with Butch, and not one time had I had an inkling that he was sick.

Not only that, my husband had promised me he would live to be a hundred and twenty five years old. He'd promised me we would grow old together. *Now he was gone*. I was so hurt; I felt like he'd lied to my face. Looking back, I think Butch had known he would be gone, but he hadn't wanted to alarm me.

Every chance I got, I would peek at his friends to see how

they were holding up, and none of them were doing that well. They were just there to pay respects to their friend. As for me, I was functioning, but I had been in a state of shock since Butch had slipped away from me and the children.

Ahhh, my children … I knew I needed to be strong for them, especially for my son. That was why at the funeral I didn't want anyone doing any unnecessary hugging or talking to make me sad.

After the viewing was over, my sister gave the eulogy. Then it was on to the gravesite, where the May sun was shining and the grass was just greening up. As I think back on it, I realize it was ironic; there we were in the spring-time, with everything coming alive, and my husband was dead. Through my haze of shock and grief I saw blue skies and clouds. There were lines and lines of cars, as far as the eye could see. If I hadn't known better, I would have thought we were burying a celebrity.

Finally we arrived at the gravesite. I got out of the car and the kids followed my lead. Wearing a shoe with a not-too-high heel that pierced the earth below me, we headed toward the bier where I could see my husband's costly, shiny, baby blue casket in the distance. Once we neared it, we would await the final word.

I really didn't want to go, but the closer we got, the harder I fought to hold back tears. I did so in the attempt to remain composed for my children. As I walked, I was thinking that as a minister, I had given eulogies and performed funerals for other grieving families, but this time was different. It was, for me, because I was burying *my* husband.

In the chairs that were there, I sat with my children, lost, and not knowing what I would do after the funeral. There was a gun salute and officers were clicking their heels. Seated beside my son, I knew Butch was being honored but I couldn't help but feel as though things were taking too long. To make matters worse, the airmen and officers that were saluting me with my husband's flag—because he had been in the Air Force—seemed to also take forever. Yet they finally got to me and delivered the folded flag. I was glad that part was over, but on some level I realized that now I would have to deal with the aftermath…

When the preacher spoke the final prayer over my husband, ending with *ashes to ashes, dust to dust*, it was time to get back into the family limo. I was still stunned and unable to believe that my husband was gone, *forever*. I simply could not grasp that I would never see Butch again. I just stood there a minute trying to take it all in. I tried to make sense of everything that had taken place, but I couldn't.

I had been to many funerals, but never to one that had left me nearly numb with grief as well as disbelief. Really, I just wanted everyone else to leave the cemetery and let me stay a little longer. To me things felt so unreal. I couldn't wrap my mind around the fact that Butch was gone…because we had just had an in-depth conversation a few nights earlier, and at that time nothing had seemed out of place.

Thank God it was a sunny day because my husband's casket was left on top of the ground. I had been told it would stay there until the workers got his grave ready. Feeling unspeakably sad, I left a single red rose on Butch's casket. I couldn't believe I was leaving him in the cemetery, by himself. I wondered whether birds or squirrels or even a stray dog would come and bother him. I didn't want that.

The limo took me and my kids back to the house, and all I could think was *Lord, help me get through this pain*, for the sake of my children. Back at my house which was crowded, everybody was talking, eating and laughing about the Butch they remembered. I really wasn't concerned at the time about how people remembered my husband. Really, I just wanted everybody to leave so that I could grieve, in peace. I wanted to be able to sort things out without all that noise.

Finally, in groups people started to leave. When the last group left I was happy, and sad, for I would be free to grieve, but I felt as if I had already cried a river of tears that day and before. They were tears that no one but God and I knew about.

The next few days and weeks were horribly lonely and sad, because I had no idea where my kids and I would end up. I only knew one thing for sure. I couldn't stay in our house. There were too many memories and no Butch to go with them, so that was too much to bear.

In a few weeks I made the decision to get rid of the house and move into something smaller. I found a townhouse a few blocks away. I got a moving truck, and all I can remember is that I just started to throw things in boxes, and in the trash. Back when my husband had bought the big house for me, for my birthday, I never dreamed I would be walking away from it just three and a half short years later. I was devastated, but I knew I had to let go.

The kids and I moved to the townhouse and settled in, but day in and day out, I would just sit and cry. However, I would never let my son see me. Although now that I think about it, he had to know because children know more than adults give them credit for.

My dog Crystal was so much of a comfort to me back then. She knew I was sad. Every evening too, she would sit by the door, just waiting for Butch to show up. She did this day in and day out for many weeks. My poor dog listened for the sound of my husband's car, but when he never showed up, she had to realize—like I did—that he wasn't coming back.

The old saying is a dog is a man's best friend, but in my case, that beautiful golden dog was this woman's best friend. For many years after Butch's death, Cocker Spaniel Crystal was my friend. I took her for her daily walks, and that was when I did a lot of my writing.

When Crystal finally got that Butch was gone, forever, she stayed close to me, to make sure I was okay. That dog is the reason why to this day I am a lover of dogs, because once they become part of your family they won't allow anybody to get near you if they think that person will harm you.

I will always remember my dog Crystal. She was a friend of mine. She was the same for my kids, for a long time.

Lord knows I needed her.

7 / THE AFTERMATH

The morning after the funeral everything started to sink in... Butch was gone and he wasn't coming back. He would not be getting up to go to the Post Garage, the auto mechanic shop on Fort Belvoir.

There was no need for me to fix tea for him, no need to prepare his lunch either, anymore. I still can't believe that man drank tea; most men drink coffee. Yet my Butch was no longer going to be around, not even to cook for his friends at work. He had always looked forward to cooking lunch. Lots of days he'd grilled stuff at his job and his friends loved his cooking. As little as is said about it, Butch and his cooking are the reason my son cooks.

Back then I realized I could no longer go to my husband's job to tease him, as I often had in the past. While Butch lived, I would just stop by the garage. Now there would be no more of that, and no more outings at the race track with our son. I kept thinking... There would be no more cookouts or pool parties in the back yard. Why? Because Butch was gone, and that was all there was to it.

I allowed the kids to return to school on a Monday. In the meantime, I also had to keep Nahum busy, so I let him continue to work at the shop that I'd bought just five months earlier. The girls seemed to be okay, but they had their terrible moments too. My poor Yolanda even felt it was her fault that her dad had died. There was just a dark cloud and sadness that hung over our house on Duran Drive.

Two of my sisters had gotten married at my and Butch's home and although my kids and I had moved to another house after his passing, memories still lingered with us. There is just no way fourteen years worth of memories can vanish in just a few days.

To me it didn't matter how I felt about Butch's sudden death, the truth was: I never wanted my kids to know that I was struggling as hard as I was to deal with it. So I buried myself in work. I did it so I wouldn't have to think about how quickly my husband had gone. He had been a certified auto mechanic that knew cars inside and out. He was the best mechanic I have ever known. That is why it took me a long time to accept the fact that he had been able to work on those cars, every day, turning all kind of wrenches and machinery, but still he hadn't wound up sick nor had he passed out. But then again, maybe he'd hid that from me too…

After the funeral I received a copy of the autopsy. I was shocked to find out that my husband had been seeing a doctor, privately, at his job. Butch used to tell me that his friend 'Dave' was seeing a doctor at the job and I believed him. When I read the autopsy, with surprise I learned that my husband had been taking a medication to freeze pain in his heart.

I was devastated once again. I was also upset with Butch for dying because he *could have* had open heart surgery to take care of the problem! He could have still been with me and the kids!

I remember that Butch had spoken to me when my dad had been sick, back when the doctors had opened my dad up. That was when my husband told me that if anything happened to him, don't let anyone operate on him. He said he just wanted to live out his days and go home. But my dad had lived one more year, when he'd only been given six months.

I had so much to deal with after my husband died because I hadn't been left with a bankroll or anything. I had a shop where I did hair, but it seemed like all the money I made, I paid out to someone or something else. It got so bad that I had to get up early in the mornings to go to another city just to stand in line to get money to pay my bills. I also had to get bags of food to feed my kids. As bad as things had gotten, I didn't even qualify for welfare, help from the county. Anyway, when I would receive food from charity, I'd always make it back home, even if my car would sometimes break down. I would just get a jump from somebody. But where was Butch? That was what I thought, because I needed him. I would get home just in time to fix breakfast before the kids would get up for school, so you know I had been out extra early. My kids had no idea that I was struggling, mentally as well as financially. I kept this from them. I didn't want to burden them because they were young. All they knew was that there was always food to eat. I was in pain but I never let them know. I especially didn't want my son to know, because he had been so sad when we lost his dad.

I just wanted this phase of the dream—the *nightmare*, really—to be over, but the truth was…it wasn't a dream or a nightmare; either of those I could have awakened from. This I lived, whether I was asleep or awake.

Although I'm not proud of it, it took me ten years to be able to go anywhere near the cemetery where my husband was buried. After Butch's death, I didn't want any parts of any of the type of foods we had shared together either. Many things were just too painful to deal with. Well anyway, ten years passed and I finally got the strength to go to his gravesite. But before I went, I decided to stop by the florist and pick up his favorite flowers.

As I was riding to the site, I was thinking about what Butch might say to me about taking so long to visit him. You see, you may not understand what I'm saying, but the truth is the spirit of a person never dies. It lives on, even after the body does not.

At the cemetery, I walked through hundreds of headstones. Finally, I reached my husband's and as I got ready to lay the flowers on his grave, a single rose broke off—without me touching it. I know that Butch's spirit was saying, 'Keep this single rose with you always.'

I announced to Butch that after I left the cemetery, I would go to the store. Yes, to buy the ingredients for a German chocolate cake. I said, "When I finish making it, and putting the icing on it, I am going to eat a piece for you, and one for me, because I know you loved German chocolate cake."

However, after that day I never made another one of those cakes. Some of our other favorite foods I still rarely eat.

At the cemetery, when I visited, I told my son's father, the love of my life, that I was sorry that I was just getting to see him, but I had not been able to handle visiting at the time; it had just been too much. Unless you've walked a mile in my shoes—the painful shoes of losing a husband or a loved one—I don't really expect you to know how I feel, but death is death, no matter what.

Away from the cemetery, while waiting for things to pick up at the salon; meaning I needed more customers, I found myself taking many walks with Crystal, my dog. I would write poems. The main reason I became a poet was because I had been so devastated when my husband died. I didn't know what to do, or how to feel, so I decided to put my feelings on paper. The first two poems I dedicated to my husband, you will be able to read one at the end of this chapter; but at the time, I had no idea that I would write another eight hundred.

During my beginning phase, a lot of my poems were about the pain of losing my husband, and about how I dealt with my new life as a widow. There was a time that I didn't have much money to buy food either, so I wrote about that. During those bleak days I always told myself "If I survive this, I will survive anything." And I did just that. However, during my hardest times, what devastated me more than anything was that none of Nahum's uncles came to see about us. My brothers, nor Butch's brothers, cared enough to see if I needed a hand with my eleven year old son. To this day, my son is sometimes still bothered by that. Boys need positive male figures in their lives and my son was no different. But since not one of his uncles offered a hand, I did what I do best, even now... I persevered. I knew I couldn't be my son's father, but I prayed to God and asked Him to help me steer my son in the right direction, and God did.

My son also had a praying grandma, and six aunts. Had my youngest brother been alive, I know he would have spent time with his nephew. I appreciate the prayers of my family.

Those meant more to me than anything. Later though, my son told me that he got a lot of answers from the hood. Even today, he mentions to me how he didn't appreciate his uncles not helping him; that really hurt.

When my son was born I began taking him to church. I have always taught him about God. I reared his sisters who are a little older than he is the same way. Still, when I attended the Pentecostal church, I felt they put too much emphasis on outside stuff, like what a person wore, instead of focusing on inside things, things that matter. I felt they didn't have to act like that. As far as I am concerned, bothering people about their clothing, instead of speaking to them about changing their ways or their heart is backward. It's like catching a fish by the tail, instead of catching it with a hook in the mouth. There are other little bones of contention I have, but those I will leave alone.

If I'd known some of what I know now, back then, I would have raised my kids a little differently. Still, I can't be too upset because my son tells the world that I gave him a good foundation, with church and all, and that makes me feel proud. I was the best mentor that my son could have. I tried to be, because I wanted him to grow up to be something. I always told him and his sisters that whatever they wanted to do in life, I would support them. I said "Just don't use God's name in vain."

When Butch had been gone on for a while, my daughter got a bit on the rebellious side, hanging out with a drug dealer, the beady-eyed character that I mentioned before…and she paid for it. So did the entire family.

Beady-Eyes hung around and caused all kinds of trouble. Still, he soon found out that he could have been the king-pin of the city and it would not have mattered to me; *I* wasn't afraid of him. Maybe that was the reason why he was so disrespectful to me.

I remember…back while my husband lived, one night Butch loaded his double barrel shot gun and was going to blow that guy down our street in pieces. At the time, Beady-Eyes called our home talking junk again, and I warned him. I said "If you love life, you had better pick my daughter up around the corner, because if you pull up in front of this door, you won't see tomorrow." I knew that young man was stupid, but I wasn't sure whether he was stuck on stupid or not so I prayed. I asked God to bring a sleeping spell on my husband, because he didn't like the way Beady-Eyes disrespected me and things could have gotten so much uglier, really fast. The truth was my husband kept his shotgun loaded, and it stayed that way until he died.

I'll admit I don't like guns, but after Butch's death, if I had needed to use his gun on Beady-Eyes, it would simply have been self-defense. Why? That character was a problem, and he threatened my daughter. People, listen. When someone tells you something like what he told her, pay attention. Beady-eyes said if my daughter left him and found someone else he would kill her, and her new boyfriend. If not for prayer, he might have.

Yes, as you can imagine, after my husband's death Beady-Eyes was hanging around, becoming more and more stupid. I guess he wanted me to become afraid of him, but when it comes to protecting my children, there isn't a scared bone in my body.

I tell you, I kept that shotgun loaded, and I kept on praying. With much prayer and supplication, that character finally disappeared from our lives, but just before he did, he pulled one last stunt of many… He staged his own 'death.' It was stupid. Butch was still alive then and Beady-Eyes had some-one call our house to say that he was dead, on Constitution Avenue. However, someone else called a few minutes later and said Beady-Eyes was on Independence Avenue. Sick of the stupidity, I asked the caller, "Why [does] the body keep moving?"

After that, Beady-Eyes vanished into another state. My prayers had caused it to be so, and boy was I glad! I didn't need any more struggles. I was having enough of them already, just trying to keep my kids out of harm's way while I ran my beauty salon. Then I had to deal with my son who was still hurt over his father's death. He had developed chest pains. Nahum had actually started thinking *he* was going to die, like his dad. Not having much money, I still had to take him to the doctor, to relieve his fears.

My middle daughter went to a fashion college after she graduated from high school. Then that girl was calling home wanting to know how to cook certain foods so I gave her many cooking lessons over the phone. She was having the time of her life, and I thought she was going to wind up a fashion designer. I felt everything was going well, until my girl came home one weekend and got involved with someone much older than she…and ended up with child.

There I was, thinking she was back in school, studying hard to become a great fashion designer, but instead she called and said she'd had a dream. In it she and I were in a store shopping, and we were both with child. I told my daughter right then, "*I* am not with child!" I said, "I can't have kids…I can't get pregnant—by—myself!" I reminded her that there are no more Virgin Mary's. So I asked her was she with child, and she said yes.

I couldn't say anything. I just went numb. *That* I didn't need. I already had enough to deal with, trying to keep my son from the streets, and now this. So I asked what she wanted to do. She replied, "Come home." I wasn't pleased, at all, because I knew I would have to deal with her, and with a baby, when it arrived.

We got through it though. My daughter is doing great, raising her teenaged son, working and going to school. Both of my daughters are beautiful, inside and out, but I will tell you. So many things have happened since my husband's death.

Months before Butch passed however, I had opened my beauty salon. You know this. What I didn't tell you was that Butch had said he didn't want to be out front, just in the background, as my silent partner. I didn't mind. I was just so happy for him to be part of what I was doing. My salon's name was *Pfelt's Hair Design* (like Felt's, but the P is silent). Butch and I came up with the name together, because we both worked with our hands; I was a beautician and he was a mechanic.

His dream, as he told it to me, was to also have a *Pfelt's II Race Team.* I told him that he would get that and that I would help him, because at that time, I wanted to race cars too. He always teased me by saying I would make a great race car driver because I was heavy on my feet.

Butch always took me and Nahum to the track to watch all those race cars. My son and I were fascinated by them. The weekend before Butch died, he had taken Nahum to the race track, and he bought me a pink Playboy bunny race track t-shirt. He bought Nahum a special t-shirt too. My husband bought himself a black race tee. Those things may seem little, to you, but I will cherish thoughts of them for the rest of my life.

After my husband's passing, I buried myself in work, day after day, so that I wouldn't have to think about him dying young and so suddenly, without warning. But I couldn't forget that since Butch hadn't got a chance to wear his t-shirt, I'd decided that the next best thing would be for me to bury him in it; I didn't want him getting cold down there by himself. For his burial I also made sure he was dressed in the suit that we'd gotten married in. I supplied underwear and socks too. To me, it was all necessary even though I knew that after the funeral no one would see his smiling face any more.

My husband's death hit me like a large bolt of lightning, over and over again. It felt like when lightning knocks a house off its foundation. Everything had happened so quickly until I had no time to think or do anything but wonder why it happened at all. Each time I thought about it, I remembered how my mind had started to race, right after I got the news. Even though Butch's death hadn't been confirmed, yet I'd had a gut feeling that my sweetheart was gone, forever. I told you that immediately I began to drift into a state of shock, and that I stayed that way during the entire preparation for the funeral.

After leaving the hospital on that fateful day, when I got back to my salon calls started to come in, one after the other. At the time I didn't know how a certain man knew anything about my husband's death, but later, I found out that my mom had given him the number. She did because I had known him since I was thirteen years old. This man was respected in the community. He had his own cement finishing business. Back in the day he had been the same young man who'd wanted to marry me, a teenager, and sweep me off my feet. So there he was, years later, calling to offer me his condolences.

Mr. Cement said if I needed anything he was only a phone call away. I told him I would call him if need be, but I never did, even though I had to accept food from charity and although my car was constantly breaking down. Many days when I went to my salon, I felt so empty. I was having all kinds of emotions twisting inside of me. Now I realize that back then what I'd really needed was to stay home for more than a week, but at the time I couldn't afford to. I had a salon to run. As the owner, I needed to be there every day. Looking back, that was a long hard period, after I buried my husband.

As I think back, I realized my husband had been so happy to have bought me a house for my birthday. He truly loved my girls too, although they weren't his biological daughters. He treated them the same as he did his own sons, but the girls really hated the summer months. They didn't want to go to his favorite place, Point Lookout. He would go fishing, and I would remain on the playground with

the kids. Then later on we would see crayfish as we
walked along the beach's sandy shore.

Butch had been happy being a father, and I can't forget
that he'd said he would be around for a hundred and twenty five years. We were supposed to grow old together.
Thinking about those things made me recognize the exact
time that everything began to unravel. It had been during
the Saudi Arabian crisis, when many of America's servicemen who were younger than Butch and I were sent overseas.

At that time my husband was working at the Post Garage,
where our national forces got their cars serviced. When the
U.S. was asked for help because Iraqi troops were massed
along the Saudi Arabian border, a host of U.S. military
people were sent overseas. At home in the U.S. there were
hardly any cars to service. So since Butch and I had recently bought our house, trying to keep the mortgage paid
became hard. We became victims of bad timing. I firmly
believe that if the crisis in the Gulf would not have arisen,
my husband might have lived longer.

Butch had told no one he was sick, but after the Gulf War
began, things felt like they were closing in on us. The reason I know that the crisis was the straw that broke the
camel's back is because Butch died two years later. I
wasn't really worried about my girls after his death, but I
was concerned about my son, because he had been so close
to his dad. Butch had taken Nahum to work with him on
weekends. I'll always remember that my boy had been so
happy to be with his dad. He would also play with a little
yellow car that he loved.

Back then Butch would teach our son things, even about
cars. They were the types of things that would help Nahum
as he got older. Then after my husband died, I discovered
that he had taught our son so many things about life. When
Butch was gone and things would stop functioning, my
son would always be nearby to lend a hand. Once when

my car radio stopped functioning, my son said, "Mom, don't worry, Dad taught me how to wire a radio." I think that's why my son wanted to become an electrical engineer, and he would have been a good one.

In time, after Butch's death Mr. Cement began to call me. He was the man who had his own cement finishing business, the one who'd wanted to sweep me off my feet and marry me so long ago. Well now, he wanted to take me out, but I hesitated. I was afraid—I felt like my husband hadn't been in the ground that long!

Aware of this, Mr. Cement was respectful, he never disrespected me in any way, but he said, "You got away once, so I'm not letting you out of my sight again."

My son was young at the time, and he did need a father figure to help me finish raising him, and he liked Mr. Cement. So we started to see each other. Mr. Cement even talked about getting married.

I began to plan our wedding. I would have six to eight ballerinas, dancing down the aisle while *Overjoyed* by Stevie Wonder played. Mr. Cement wanted to sing *Dream Lover* by Mariah Carey, but nobody knew a thing about the wedding except for us.

Every day I would stand in my mirror practicing singing *Overjoyed*, because this was our second chance to get to spend eternity together. I knew Mr. Cement loved me, because he'd waited, and I must have loved him. Maybe the love was deep, deep inside of me and I didn't realize it, but I will tell you about that in my other book. However, with the normalcy of us spending time together, and with all the things he could have given me and my children, one big problem stood out... Mr. Cement was an alcoholic.

I couldn't see putting myself or my children through that. There was no way I was going through that again; I had been raised with an alcoholic father, and it had not been a pretty life. When I'd been young, most kids looked forward to the weekend; me too, but not for the same reason as the other kids. They looked forward because their dad would be home, and they could do things with him. I looked forward because my father would *not* be home, and we could have some peace. As a young lady, I became a cheerleader, a dancer, and I ran track—just anything to get out of the house, because back then my dad, who drank, was off the chain. Anyway, with my decision not to marry cemented, I went on. A while after Butch passed, I actually ended up marrying someone else, and Mr. Cement did

too, but he married on the rebound and was very unhappy. Still, when I spoke to him, I told him to try and stick it out, but he would hear none of that. He said he wanted to leave town, with me, but that never happened and Mr. Cement wound up dying a tragic death.

Upon finding out, I called his widow. She then told me, "I finally get a chance to hear your voice." She also said, "All he talked about was how he still loved you, and how he wanted to marry you." Mr. Cement's wife even said that seventy-five percent of his demise had been her; she'd worried him to death, and twenty-five percent had been worries from his job.

Of course I was devastated. I cried harder than his widow had ever thought about crying. I felt like Mr. Cement had died with a broken heart because we'd never hooked up. I asked his widow if she would send me a couple of programs from his funeral service, and she said she would.

Now I'll tell you something strange. One day I had been out driving. At the time, I didn't know Mr. Cement's funeral service was going on at a particular church that I passed. I only knew that there were so many cars in the parking lot. Seeing that as I drove by, I said, "Whoever's funeral that is, that person had a lot of friends."

A week later I found out it had been my friend. Thank God I hadn't stopped and gone in that church, because if I'd seen Mr. Cement lying in a coffin I don't know how I would have handled it. It probably would have taken me back to that awful place I'd been in immediately after the kids and I had lost Butch – for whom I wrote the following poem...

~ THAT MAN ~

Frances Wellington

He came into my life like a quiet rain,

And from that day on, nothing was ever the same.

He only wanted to love me forever and a day.

He was like a dream come true,

And everything was so brand new.

He helped to shape my life you see,

He helped me to be all I could be.

He was a loving husband and a constant friend,

But it all one day came to an end.

He was very honest, and oh so fair,

That's one thing I will declare.

He never stopped, even when he was tired,

He wanted to keep our love alive.

Even though he's at rest my friend,

I wish this day had never been.

When he departed that morning he gave me a
stare with his eyes,

But at the time

I didn't know he was saying good-bye.

God placed him in my life for fourteen years,

But after all was said and done, he disappeared.

Out of my life just like he came,

As if he was a quiet rain.

He will always have a place in my heart,

Even though we are miles apart...

Raising J. Holiday, A Mother's Untold Story

8 / HE WAS GROWING

As my son got older, people started envying him, for many reasons. Some of them included the fact that he was light-skinned, with braids, and had a car. I was the one who'd begun braiding his hair, and he bought his car with his own money. The real trouble began when he entered high school and decided he wanted to become a singer. Some guys said he was taking all the girls from them. My son couldn't help it if he was nice-looking and popular with girls—he always had been.

My son had friends who had a studio and they knew he sang. Once my son realized he wanted to sing for a career, he stayed at the studio, working on tracks, sometimes into the wee hours of the morning. I wasn't worried about him, because there were older guys that would look out for him. As a mother, I had to let him grow and be his own man. Still, the closer it got to him graduating, the more I prayed for God to prepare me for his leaving, and God did just that.

But before graduation, there was always some drama going on, at the high school. It was usually about nothing at all, but seemed like certain guys were determined to pick fights with my son and his step-brother. Once, these kids got the notion to come to my house to fight my son. At the time, I didn't know that my son's so-called best friend was in on the set-up, but what 'best friend' didn't know was that I was home that night.

I remember… My son and his step-brother were in my son's room. I leaned in and asked, as I usually did, was everything alright. Nahum said yes, they were just talking about girls. That didn't set right with me though, maybe because they'd answered so quickly. Yet I realized I was a little on the restless side, so I went outside to throw some-thing away. That's when I saw about sixty boys crowded into the parking lot beside my house. The thing was: my car wasn't in the lot so those boys had thought I wasn't home.

By that time my son had come outside, ready to battle, and thank God I was present because I know if I hadn't been, it would have become a bloodbath; I told you the story earlier in this book. Then the world would never have heard of *J. Holiday*. I am so grateful God was with us that night.

The following morning in October 1998, I went to the high school to transfer my son out of there. I enrolled him in the school where I was teaching. I was determined that the rest of his school year would be peaceful, but boy was I wrong! As soon as I got Nahum transferred, the trouble started, *again*, in the new school. This time, a career criminal's girlfriend claimed my son was flirting with her, while her man was in jail. When Criminal was released, he came straight to the school to see his girlfriend, Ms. Thing. So you know she told him.

One day my son was at lunch and that young man, Criminal, tried to take my son's car. Nahum had a time, his last year in school! I didn't understand it then, but I do now. He was on his way to his destiny, and at every turn someone was trying to stop him. That young man, Criminal, finally got banned from the school campus, but one day he came back with a group of boys—to beat on my son. I had just arrived at the school and had no idea who the young man was, but I heard him mention my son's name. I turned right around and reported him to the authorities and he was arrested before my eyes.

This kind of stupidity went on for another three to four months, until finally my son wanted to squash things once and for all. He wanted to fight, but before he threw the first blow, he wanted to know why Criminal disliked him; Criminal's piss-poor reason? He thought my son was in a gang. Really dumb.

Finally, my son was able to finish school, and *graduate*, in peace.

9 / PFELT'S HAIR DESIGN

Long before my son got to high school or got his first car, and long before he died, my husband Butch, the kids, and I, had been in our house about two years and there was still more to accomplish. I was working as a manager at one of the biggest chain salons, but I would always tell my husband that I was not going to work for anyone for the rest of my life. I was going to work for myself, and I was determined not to work for the white man. Not that I was prejudiced, I simply felt that way because when I had been a little girl, I had seen my parents go through so many struggles with them, and I was determined that I wouldn't repeat my parents' life.

I had no idea when or where I would get my salon, but in my mind I always saw it, in the distance. I knew if I kept focused, my dream would one day become reality. I knew it because while I worked at the chain salon I was learning a lot, and much of it was about running a business. That's why I felt like when opportunity knocked, I would be ready. I would see what it would feel like to own something.

At the chain salon where I was manager, one of the stylists told me of an independent salon that was for sale in the suburbs. Then one day she and I went together to take a look. The owner showed us the salon he was selling, but although I wanted to, I still felt like it wasn't the time for me to purchase. I thanked my stylist for telling me about the place and for going with me, but I also explained to her what I felt. Still, I had no idea that two weeks later, I would get a leading deep in my gut—an unmistakable feeling—to go back to the suburban salon, alone. Not only did I purchase it, but I got it for twelve thousand dollars less than the asking price! I was so happy to be a new salon owner. I walked in a stylist and walked out an owner.

There's more to come about that in the book about my life.

When I told my husband what took place, he and I imme-diately came up with the name Pfelts (pronounced Felts) Hair Design because we both worked with our hands; we felt things. Anyway, I had become a salon owner over-night! My son, who was about eight at the time, was so happy because he had always visited the other shop where I had only been the manager. Now he would really get to see what it was like for his mother to be her own boss.

It was amazing, the way I had been able to purchase that salon—with no money, but it was my time, and nothing was able to stand in my way. God had made it so that the seller didn't even ask me for any money down. I was simply able to start making payments a few months later. I officially opened on Valentines' Day 1993. The night before, my husband and Nahum thoroughly cleaned the shop.

When I became the owner, I was determined to be the best business owner in that shopping mall. The reason I wanted this was because I knew the company that I had just left was watching me. I was now their competition, but I was not bothered a bit. Matter of fact, some of their stylists came on board with me—even though I had not solicited them. Those stylists just made up their own minds. They wanted to work for me.

I also knew that if I wanted my children to be responsible, then I had to be their best role model. I always told my children that whatever type of job they had, they had to do it well. Since I had been working at one of the top salon chains in the area, I already had knowledge of how to run a salon. I had big plans for my future, and none of those plans included working for Miss Ann.

I had people from all walks of life working for me, and I gave all the salons in that area a run for their money, in-cluding the one where I'd received my training. I hired all of my children; I mentioned it before, and gave each one their own responsibilities. If they didn't do what they had been hired to do, they didn't get a paycheck. Determined to turn that salon around, I wanted to give it the best makeover that I could.

My son Nahum stayed busy keeping the salon swept and free of fallen or cut hair. Sometimes he would do extra tasks so he could get more money to buy candy, or so he could play video games. My girls stayed busy too, doing manicures and answering the phone. Then after his dad's sudden death, I kept my son busy so he wouldn't have time to feel sad.

I remember one Saturday…his little self wanted to go play video games with some kids who were getting bored while waiting for their mom to get her hair done. My son was supposed to have been sweeping up hair off the floor, but he was talking about playing.

I told him he could make his own choice; either stay and work, or go and play. But, I said, if he went to play, he was not getting paid for that day. Since that was pay day, he received his envelope later on, as usual. However, when he looked inside and began to count his money, he got a surprise. He was missing a day! He looked at me with a sad face. I felt bad, but I had to do it. I said, "You thought I was playing. I told you if you went to play video games I wasn't going to pay you." I had to teach him a lesson. I wanted to give him the correct work ethic. Since he no longer had a dad, it fell to me to do so.

On the whole, I would be occupied from the time I got to work until I left, and that was late, so that when I returned home I could only go to bed and sleep. Then I would do it all over again the next day. I was counseling everybody too; stylists, patrons, and even homeless people, but my kids and I were the ones who really needed counseling, after what we had been through.

This went on for a year after my husband's death, until one day I just couldn't take it anymore. I had to take time, for me. I had to grieve. My son wouldn't talk a lot about his dad's death, but I knew he was sad too. I knew that sometimes it could take years of tears and sadness to deal with something that drastic and sudden.

Even with an unsure future for my son, I knew we would somehow make it. I have always been a strong person and have never wanted anyone to see me sweat. I was the boss. This I told myself, therefore, my son didn't need to see me crying. That was the reason I always hid my hurt and tears, and my son did the same. I felt like I didn't want to let my kids down, or any of my employees. So I faced life head-on.

As I did, I was yet filled with sorrow, year after year. Then one day I met a young man that brought me pure joy, and I forgot my pain. I would find out many years later though that all he did was enable my pain to lie dormant. This man became my friend, and a role model for my son. He was so much like Butch that it was like my husband had never left my life. This new man was a Butch lookalike, to me. He even had the same birthday. As far as I was concerned, I had hit the jackpot. As long as he was in my life, I reasoned, I didn't have to deal with pain.

But…there came a time when he abandoned me, and the pain of losing Butch resurfaced. It was something that I had to deal with. It was not easy, because the pain of loss had been lying dormant for eight years. It had been undisturbed, but when that pain was finally probed, there were layers upon layers of disappointment as well.

10 / ADVERSITY

I was trying very hard to deal with my husband's death, and I will tell no one that it was anything close to being easy. That's why I keep mentioning it.

To deal with things, my kids and I moved from the big house we'd shared with Butch, to a townhouse not more than five minutes away. Still every day I would go past our old home, to get a look and take a few pictures because I was really struggling, physically and mentally with many things.

Then on December thirty-first, the end of the year, on the way home from the store my daughters had an accident! They weren't hurt, but my car was, and I had no funds to fix it. Still, I told the kids that we were going to church on New Year's Day. Dealing with the rattling car, we set out for church that Sunday. I was determined to see what the New Year's message would be.

Well we got safely to the church. I was so glad to be in the house of the Lord. As my kids and I sat down I began to praise the God of our salvation. As the choir was singing *There's Nobody Greater Than God* I sat there thinking about me being alone, and about the death of my husband which was still fresh in my soul. Still, I gave out the biggest yes to God. I was saying yes Lord, to His will, and yes to His way. I had no idea what I would do or how my little family would make it, but deep in my gut I knew the Lord was with us.

That Sunday the Bishop preached the greatest message, and I needed every word. The message was: *Have faith and believe only; no matter the task*. After the service was over, those words became Rhema words to me—words that are extremely timely and valuable in a Christian's life.

After I'd greeted the Bishop and the first lady and a few other members, my children and I headed home. On the way, I decided to stop by my mom's house. As we were driving along, I could only think *Have faith and believe only;* no matter what.

When we arrived at my mom's no one was home, but I had a key so we went in. I told the kids to get a snack and watch a little TV. While they were busy, I decided I would clean my mom's house. It wasn't dirty but I needed to do something, at least for a few minutes in the hope that I wouldn't think about my husband…but to no avail.

While I was cleaning I heard an evil voice say I'd better stop cleaning because "That's what happened to your husband... He was cleaning everything, then he died." I stood right in my tracks and rebuked that evil voice. I commanded it to leave my presence.

I finished the cleaning and we left. On the way home, my kids and I were talking about the service. They also mentioned their feelings about things like our life at the time, and about having moved from the big house. My son always wanted to ride shot-gun, no matter what, and we had been riding and talking for about twenty minutes when I immediately heard a still small voice instruct me to tell my son to put his seatbelt on. I did.

In the back, my grandbaby, my daughter's baby was crying. Now usually when we were so close to home I would allow my daughter to get her baby out of the little seat and hold her the remainder of the way. However, that night was different because I wouldn't allow it. I was going back and forth with God and Satan, and of course God won the battle.

Just before I was about to take my exit, all I could see ahead were bright lights. I realized the cars before me were stopped, so I stopped—and was hit real hard from the back! Our old car spun around and around, again and again! All I could remember was gripping the steering wheel and thinking *have faith and believe only...* Inside I was praying while we were spinning around. I was asking God not to let anyone involved get seriously hurt, and God was with us, even when my car was being hit from behind.

It turned out to be a nine-car pile up, with my car being the fifth, all because a drunk driver had gotten out of his vehicle. He'd left it in the road and had never returned. That was the cause of all the cars on top of each other. I was thankful that I know the voice of the Lord, and that I had obeyed when I'd heard his voice.

When my car stopped spinning it was turned sideways. Before the rescue squad arrived, there were people running over. A couple looked in and said, "Be thankful you have this type of car," they named it, then they claimed "because it saved you all's life."

I looked those people square in the face and said "This may be a good car, but *it* didn't save our lives; *Jesus* did." After that statement the woman became quiet.

When the rescue squad arrived, they had to put a blanket on me with my hurt neck, and on my son. They also had to break my front windshield, because my middle child, my daughter, was stuck in back of my car. I sat holding my twelve-year old son's hand beneath our borrowed blanket. I did it to give him comfort. We watched too as that night my Volvo became a convertible.

The rescue workers got my baby daughter safely out and put her in their vehicle. For our one family alone there were three rescue squads. I will never forget it, because to me it still feels like it was only yesterday that all of this happened. My son and I rode in the same rescue squad, side by side, holding hands and I kept telling him that everything would be okay.

However, I know the enemy never stops. I know too that the devil was trying to take my entire family out that day. Trust me. Yet I am happy to say that seventeen years later all is well. My son could have been thrown through the front windshield, had I not obeyed God and told Nahum to buckle up, but *today* he is a famous R&B singer, all over the world. My daughter, the one that they had to cut from the rear of the car is now a teacher who has her Bachelor's Degree. My eldest daughter is now married and working for a non-profit foundation. Once she supplied backing vocals for the artist Crystal Waters, but now she's working steadily on her own album. And yours truly has become an ordained minister. I am also a writer, a children's-book illustrator, a poet, a teacher, and so much more.

God is good, and faithful. My grand-daughter who was about eight months old at the time is now a high school graduate. At the time of this writing, she is on her way to Manhattan to attend Marymount University where she will major in Political Science and Theater.

Following that accident, our family faced many challenges, but none of them were worthy of us quitting. I told you, I am one who perseveres, and I have taught my kids and grandkids to do the same.

11 / MORE DISTRACTIONS

After my husband's passing I was trying to get myself together so I could continue to raise my children. I was having a hard enough time functioning after such a devastating blow so I certainly didn't need any other distractions that might cause me to lose focus even more…

Well, by the time of which I speak, my son was in junior high, where he rode a bus to school every day. That worked out because each day I could go to my salon. There I kept things running smoothly so that I could continue paying bills and taking care of my two minor kids.

Each day my son rode the bus to school and he rode it

home. One evening, I got a call from his school. What I was basically being told was that he could no longer ride the school bus. Why? The lady bus driver had reported my son. I was told he had been caught hanging his head out of the window. As if that wasn't bad enough, she said he was cursing at people as the bus passed them by.

You talk about snapping? I did just that! I told the principal, "You are not taking my son off the bus." I said so because he would have had no way to get to school. I also mentioned that I had a business to run, and I had to be there every day. I demanded a meeting, the next morning, with the principal, the assistant principal, the bus driver, the assistant bus driver, *and* the school superintendent.

On the phone I said, "I want the bus driver to tell me—in front of all of you—that she knew it was *my son* cursing and hanging his head out of the window." I said I would ask her, in front of everybody, if she'd had her eyes on the road and was paying attention to what was going on in front of her, then how in the hell could she know who was cursing out the window?

I told the principal that I would be there first thing in the morning. I added "If the bus driver can prove that it was my son's voice she heard, I will kiss my own foot. If she can't prove it," I warned, "she had better stop harassing my son, and simply drive that bus—*if* she values her job."

The meeting took place. As I had already known, the bus driver was unable to prove her claims. So I had no more problems out of her, not about my son riding the bus for the rest of the school year. Before we ended that meeting though, I spoke to the bus driver. I said, "Unless you are going to pick my son up every day—in your own personal vehicle—to get him back and forth to school, then don't make false statements against him."

Now that I take inventory of my son's life, I see that he has been a target for harassment as long as I can remember. I'm not saying my child is perfect, but he was no worse or no better than other kids his age. And back when he was still attending middle school, he told me that just about every day, the same bus driver who'd accused him had cussed at the kids and acted like she didn't want to drive the bus. He said she was cursing when they got on the bus in the morning and when she picked them up in the evening. That type of negativity nobody, not even kids, should have to deal with. That was why I made it my business to make sure that particular driver was removed from that bus route. She was taken away, after some time. Then for whatever reason, she was later fired.

Ladies and gentlemen, I can put up with a lot, but *not* with stupid stuff, and not when it affects me or my kids. That I won't deal with. I'm not saying my son didn't curse and hang his head out the window, because kids have been known to try all sorts of things when their parents aren't around. I know my son was just like any other kid when he wasn't around me; that I have never denied, but he has never disrespected me in front of my face. I couldn't watch my three kids twenty-four seven, but with the foundation that I laid for my girls and their brother, I expected them to know how to conduct themselves in public.

I will tell you the one thing I know for sure. My son loved to talk. I used to tell him, "Don't be the class clown." I would also say, "You've got to dare to be different." I'll admit it; I would get calls from his teacher. Other times when he got his progress reports there would be comments about him having received certain grades *because of his talking in class* when he was supposed to be listening to the teacher.

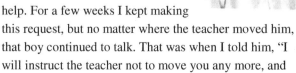

Once I asked his teacher to move him to another seat to see if that would help. For a few weeks I kept making this request, but no matter where the teacher moved him, that boy continued to talk. That was when I told him, "I will instruct the teacher not to move you any more, and the next progress report you get, the grades and the comments had better be different!"

My son finally got the point and got himself together. He knew that if I showed up at school—because he had been running his mouth in class—there would definitely be problems...between me and him.

12 / SPEAK LORD, THY SERVANT HEARETH

There came a morning when I woke and realized my husband was not coming back. Although it was summer, and beautiful outside with blue skies and green grass, the fact that Butch was gone got to me. In the townhouse where the kids and I had moved to get away from the memories at the big house, I sat on the side of my bed and found myself crying. I was so sad. If you have never lost anyone that you shared hopes and dreams with; if you've never lost anyone that you loved dearly, then you cannot understand where I was.

As I was quietly sobbing and feeling anguished, I felt like God wanted to say something to me. I felt His presence in the room. Aware of this, I got very quiet so I could hear him. I had many questions, the greatest of which was simply *why*? Therefore, I wiped my eyes and said "Speak Lord, thy servant heareth."

That was when the Lord began to reveal things to me. It was not like in the movies where a booming voice comes out of the heavens and shakes the rafters. The voice was quiet and still. The voice was not outside of me. It was inside, sort of like when you have a thought, but it was a little different. When the voice of the Lord comes to you, you know, unmistakably. You simply have to get quiet and listen for it—which is what I did that morning.

That was when the Lord let me know '*There are tasks that only your hands can perform. When you travel from the* east to the west coast and overseas, the world will know that I have sent thee.'

The Lord further spoke and said, '*Your husband loved you and was faithful. You know that, but he wanted you to be clear of all burdens, including himself. He knew the vision that was set before you, and he knew you could perform it, with or without him. So rather than hinder the vision, in any way, he asked if he could come home, to me. He didn't want to stagger the vision, not even in the smallest way. Thus, he took Early Retirement, but he will get full bene-fits.*'

The Lord also let me know… '*There are no two people alike; your husband always told you that. He was a man unlike others; a worker, a warrior, a lover, a father, a friend, and you will surely miss him. Yet he's at rest now, so don't worry about him, just do my will and I will keep my promise to you. Your husband was a man to remember, and his son will make him proud.*'

I asked the Lord why just a few years? [The length of time we'd owned our home.] His reply was, '*Your husband deserved to own a home; he had worked very hard. I had to honor your faith and his desire.*

The Lord imparted this too, '*You ask why I didn't heal him. He did not ask me to. He asked to go home. He told me why and I told you* (Butch had not wanted to stagger, or get in the way of the vision). *He was always a believer and I had to honor my word; ask and it shall be given, seek and ye shall find.*'

At the time, I had no idea how profound those words were. However, now that nearly twenty years have passed, I understand. Many things have become crystal clear. After hearing the Lord's words I felt a sense of peace. I felt like many questions had been answered. I felt an assurance that things would be okay. At that moment I was just so full that I began to cry again, but this time my tears weren't tears of sorrow.

I started feeling able to think about, and embrace my husband's short-lived but extremely full life. Now I can tell you that although the pain of losing someone never fully goes away, it does get to a point where it is manageable.

There are even times now when I think about my life with my husband and I can laugh. Other times I cry and rhetorically ask, "Butch, why'd you have to leave?" But I have accepted things. I talk to my son too sometimes, about his father. He admits that he still misses him but he deals with it, like I do. On my son's album *Back of My Lac* in the first song he speaks of losing his dad.

So you see...grief can be managed. Just trust God. He will help you. If you're in a similar situation, you'll never forget your loved one, but you won't keep drowning in sorrow.

~ B U T C H ~

Frances Wellington

Small in stature, but big in heart,

this man always did his part.

He cooked, cleaned, sewed and he ironed,

and this man was mine.

He was always a giver, and never anyone's taker,

and lord knows he wasn't a baker,

He worked hard from day to day,

he wasn't the type to waste time away.

His job was his second home,

And if he couldn't go there, he felt all alone.

Solo, I tell you in the middle of a desert,

feeling like this, he got no pleasure.

He was a loner; he didn't hang with a crowd,

and because of this he never had to bow.

13 / TOOLEY STREET

After we lost my husband, I needed to find an apartment closer to the church that I was attending at the time. The church was an hour's drive away and that was too much. It was just too far. This new church was located in Maryland. It was a wonderful word church and since my loss was still fresh, I needed to be there, in settings that would help me and my children during our healing process.

By this time I had closed the shop, my hair salon. I'd done so in February, nearly a year after my husband's passing. I felt led to close it because maintaining it was a big task and I needed to grieve without interruptions. I will explain more in another book. Remember now, I moved the kids from the home that we'd shared with Butch to a townhouse not far away. But since we were going to the wonderful word church, the one that was quite a distance away, I wound up looking at lots of places near it. I finally decided on one particular apartment complex, for many reasons. The main reason was: it was a few minutes from the church. The complex was also close to the Beltway and to shopping.

I later found out the area was very corrupt, with all types of drug activity, fighting, and kids hanging out at all times of the night. It turned out to be far beyond what I could comprehend, and I wondered why I was there, although in my heart I knew. I was there to do outreach, ministry. I also knew it certainly wasn't a place to raise my eleven year old son, but…we were there, now.

When I'd first applied at the complex, I was given an apartment right up front. I was pleased with the location, but what I did wrong was I waited a little too long to put the money down, so the manager rented the apartment to another family. I was very upset because all she had left then was an apartment way in the back, where all of the corruption went on. I told the manager that I had a young son and didn't need that apartment way back there in the boonies.

She said if I didn't take it, it would be another three whole months before another apartment would come available in the front. I should have waited. I didn't, but I did mention that I was an ordained minister and that I needed somewhere to have bible class on Wednesday night. I said if the manager could aid me with that, I would take the apartment in the back.

The manager admitted the complex needed help. She said, "If you think your ministry can help this place calm down, I will give you an extra apartment in which to have your bible classes."

That's how my kids and I wound up on Tooley, a one way street out of that apartment complex. It really was a U in shape because if you stayed on the street, you would wind up leaving right back out the same way you'd entered. My family wound up living on the cul de sac in the back, by the woods.

You'd think a cul de sac was good, right? Well it wasn't, because there was criminal activity, and back there was the criminals' hiding spot. Furthermore, it was worse because people who did wrong realized there was no road leading out from back there; but there were woods—just a whole forest full of trees and bushes for wrong-doers to hide in!

At the time, my oldest daughter wanted to bring my oldest grandchild to stay with me for a while. I wasn't excited because my daughter was still seeing Beady Eyes who'd caused problems in the past, and I didn't need his mess around my son.

Then my middle daughter decided she wanted to come home too for a while. So there we were, all in a two bedroom apartment, when the place was supposed to have only been for me and Nahum, but I would not have seen my girls in the street. So we all settled in and I began trying to clean up the place. I even wound up sleeping in the living room, when I'd had a bedroom—before my girls arrived.

When my children and I had been attending our new word church for about a year, I was still excited to have a pastor that welcomed us. Now when I first went to the church I was already rooted in ministry, but I needed leadership because I had recently become a widow. I needed help with my children, especially my son. However, the pastor of the church immediately saw God in me. He was about to start ministry school and he was choosing twelve people to participate. He had chosen eleven ministers from his congregation, but he needed one more person and that was when he looked in the audience and called me up to join the other eleven.

A few weeks went by and ministry school started. We had to go through some hard core stuff, but I made it with the help of God. I was ordained in the spring of 1995, and all my friends and family were there to cheer me on, and that was one of the happiest days of my life.

The church started to unravel about three years later… I will talk about that in my next book. Please keep your eyes out for it. However, one of my specialties has always been dealing with people whom no one else wants to deal with. Therefore, I would have bible class every Wednesday night, right across the street from my apartment. By that time I had also started to receive money from my husband's passing. Then people gave me things. They knew about my outreach ministry and that I would give away clothing and food after each session. Some of the giveaways had even been my own things but I liked being able to help the community, and I really enjoyed being near my new word church.

My son was in the ninth grade at the time, and trying his best to deal with school and the loss of his father. He was adjusting to the area quite well and meeting new friends. I would keep a close eye on him at all times though because there was so much violence around there.

It was always a little struggle for me, at least for a while, when it came to providing the things I needed for my son. When he was in the ninth grade, his class planned to take a trip to New York City for a day. Nahum was so excited about going, until every day he would talk about it. He did this until the time came to go.

I had paid the trip fee, but I knew he would still need spending money while he was out. My son had an idea that I didn't have extra money, but he wasn't aware that I really might not have a dime in time for his trip. Still, I told him that I would get it. Then my mind was racing, and I was asking, "Lord, what am I going to do?"

I realized there was another thing that I could do. I could pawn my rings! Yes, so that my son could go on his trip and have a good time, but I did not tell him this. He was a child. He didn't need my adult burdens.

Those going on the trip were scheduled to leave the school the next day around ten o'clock, so I knew I could take my rings to the pawn shop early, get money for my son to spend, and take it to the school before the bus left.

I got to the school just in time; the students might have been boarding the bus then, I don't really remember. I only know that Nahum was looking for me. I gave the money to him, and my son went to New York and enjoyed himself. I was just that good.

When he came back, he brought me something. I also remember that he'd bought some red, white, and blue shorts made of jersey material. They were special basketball shorts with some type of New York logo on them.

He loved those shorts very much. He wore them a lot.

One day I took our clothes downstairs to the laundry room. I finished washing them, but forgot they were there. A family that had moved in a month earlier had a teenage son who was always getting in some type of trouble. Of course, he went downstairs and stole my son's jersey shorts, the ones he'd gotten after I'd pawned my rings so he could have his New York trip. When my son found out his shorts were gone, he was so upset. I told him not to worry because I was going to call the police. I said if that other boy had his possessions then that kid was going to give them back, or go to jail.

When the policeman came and knocked on my door, I told him where the boy's family lived. Instead of the officer just doing his job, he came downstairs to tell me that the boy had the shorts on, plus the boy denied he'd stolen them. But earlier that day he had been bragging about the theft, and about being from New York.

I told the policeman, "I don't care. You'd better go back upstairs and tell him to take my son's shorts off—or I will do it myself!" I had my hands on my hips because I don't play, and I ain't scared of no po-po!

The officer made the boy take the shorts off and brought them back to me. I washed those shorts about five times before I allowed my son to wear them again, and from that day on, the New Yorkers in the complex realized I wasn't someone who was afraid of anybody. I was to be reckoned with. My motto has always been, don't play with me, or sleep on me when it comes to my kids or anything else that is mine.

There was another incident with one of my neighbors. This woman was a drug dealer and an addict. She asked me to take her to the store to get food for her kids, but when she was in my car, she wanted to first make a stop. Her stop was taking me to a red district, an area where people can buy drugs. At the time I didn't know, but when I realized, I told her, "I don't care if you never get food for your kids, I am never taking you anywhere else." Dealing with people like that, you can lose what you have. That woman had no regard for me or my kids. I could have gone to jail, or lost my kids to the Foster Care system, but she only wanted what she wanted.

Didn't I tell you that Tooley Street was off the chain?

Another time, a neighbor came knocking on my door because someone had sold her some soap instead of crack, and she wanted me to take her to get her money back! I looked her square in the face and said I wasn't taking her anywhere. I said if she was going to get high, it would have to be off that soap.

Tooley was a place where there was always some type of drama going on.

There was a little old raggedy basketball rim not far from the window that I could look out of and see my son. He loved to play basketball, especially with his friends. He'd met a little boy whose parent I met and I would let Nahum go play with the boy. Still, I always had to check to see where my son was. I would let him be out, not far from the house, but sometimes a few kids would try him and want to fight him. What was great was that there were bigger boys out there and they would see this. They often said they weren't going to let Nahum fight because his mother was a preacher. They would fight for him. I would also let him go to the store, but it had to be daytime, when it was light out.

In 1996 there was a big snow storm that kept us in. As soon as we thought it was over, we wound up getting about another ten to twelve inches of snow.

I had been living at the complex about six months when I met a young man called Professor. He looked so much like my husband that he scared me. I first saw him at the ice cream truck. One night I was out getting a treat for me and my dog Crystal and my boy was inside sleeping.

This man, Professor, and I talked for a little while that night. He told me about his life. I didn't ask him anything, but he just started talking to me, so I listened. After that we became good friends. Then friends turned into dating. He was a carpenter who laughed at his own jokes. He was a lot of fun to have around and I didn't really see any harm in that because my son liked him very much. My girls were a little older, so they weren't too sure about him.

One day I asked Professor if he could take me and my son to the skating rink. His reply was, "Yes, but I don't know how to skate." I said that was okay. I said, "You can watch me teach my son to skate."

When we got to the rink, my son and I were sitting there putting on our skates. I asked him had he seen the professor and he said no. We both looked up at the same time and saw Professor on the floor—skating. Surprise! Not only was he skating, but he was skating backward. So he had told us a big lie. Not that lies are funny, but we got a huge laugh out of that. After that, Professor taught my son to skate forward and backward. I was pleased with him doing that because those types of things were what I'd always wanted my husband Butch to do with the family.

I already knew how to skate, but not all that fancy stuff, not all that carrying on, so skating with Professor, often, I became a better skater. I even told him, "You can skate backward all you want, but I'll skate forward—so I can see where I'm going."

The Professor was a carpenter, and he was really good, so much so, that he taught my son how to build houses and put up drywall. They finished putting up drywall in the guest house at one of the sites that Professor was working at. My son really liked him and the work. So you see, if my son wasn't a singer he could work with his hands. He has options.

I would advise every young person to have career options.

Raising J. Holiday, A Mother's Untold Story

14 / SEQUOYAH

In the fall of September 1996 we moved to Sequoyah which was located in another state. I had just recently married Professor and I wanted a new beginning. He and I had found a place a few weeks before our wedding. He had a teenage son that he was raising, and I had my three children, one granddaughter, and another grandbaby on the way. Although I was excited about being a grand mom and about my new husband, I had never wanted to raise any children other than my own. I didn't feel like taking on a teenage son; one whom I knew nothing about and who could create a problem.

I know I was being selfish, because I was only taking on one child that wasn't mine while Professor was taking on four, plus one on the way, but that was how I felt. Anyway, Professor's son started getting on the other kids nerves the first week. Therefore, I told him he would either abide by my rules, just like my own kids, or he would go back to Maryland, "And live with your mammy." I had to set the ground rules from the start. As a matter of fact, I hadn't even known Professor had a son until a month before we married! The boy had been in the streets, trying to be a thug.

By this time, my son already knew he wanted to be a singer, so he joined every chorus group available to him. When he attended Forestville High School and sang in the talent show he got over being shy. What really helped him conquer those feelings was being chosen for a Big Brothers' program at James Madison University. After those three weeks of mentoring, my son's life became totally different; I could see it when he returned home. He was no longer the shy little boy that I'd left behind three weeks earlier. What a difference the mentoring made. My son seemed ready to tackle the world and to receive what it had to offer.

While we were settling into our new home, everyone seemed to be trying to get along with their new brother, Professor's son, but he kept some mess going. I told him that he had better glean as much as possible from me, while he was there. In truth, I gave that young man the same opportunities that I gave my own son. But what I didn't like was when the Professor and I moved there, his son's mom thought she was going to call and talk to my husband whenever she got ready. I stopped that stuff in the very beginning. I even told her that her son was not a baby, "So you will not use him just so you can talk to my husband." I was not having it. You see, when I was growing up my mom always told me "Start out like you can hold out." In other words she meant 'start as you mean to finish,' or more simply put, 'don't let people walk over you.'

There came a time when Professor's son got sick. The boy called his mom and made her think he was being mistreated. The mother said she wanted to come over and bring her son some soup, some medicine and the like, which was fine with me. But she came to my house with an attitude. She didn't know who she was dealing with. I sat her down and told her, "This is my house. If you think your son is being mistreated, in anyway, then when you go out that door you can take him with you." I also told that woman that she should be concerned about her son getting in his correct grade, so he could graduate, on time. Then I warned her not to approach me with foolishness. I was about business.

When Nahum was about fifteen years old, he was able to get his first job. Since he was so shy, I'd gone to the movie theater in the area where we lived and asked the manager if they were hiring. I told him my son needed a job. I said my son was a hard worker and was very neat. The manager told me to tell my son to come in for a full interview. Nahum went in and the manager liked him and hired him on the spot!

My son loved his new job at the theater, and because he was an usher he got to meet people. Most people that went there or worked there liked him, especially the girls.

My son knew he was good-looking, but I would still remind him so that I could see his nice smile. Still I told him, "Don't let it go to your head."

The manager that hired him was awesome, but there was another manager, one I didn't like—because he was a mean redneck. I believe he was jealous because my son was getting girls, of all races. Anyway, my son was working one night and decided to take a break, during which he was talking to the girls at the concession stand. The redneck manager barked that my son should get back on his post. My son remembered that I had always told him and his sisters to always have another job if they were going to quit their current one.

I had also said if their manager treated them like a slave, they could quit, because I had been through that. Well my son quit. When he got home a little earlier than usual, I asked why. He told me what happened. I told him that he'd done the right thing. I said I was going to speak with the manager who'd hired him. The next day I spoke with that manager. I let him know that he needed to speak to the night manager because my son knew how to carry himself. I also reminded the manager that it wasn't the sixties and my son wasn't anybody's slave. I thanked the manager for hiring my son, before I mentioned that my son wouldn't work there under those circumstances. You see my son is quiet, just like his dad, but don't back him in a corner. It's the story of the dog that corners a cat. The cat will come out fighting.

It wasn't a week before Nahum started working at a thrifty food store where he was a bagger. At times he also stocked shelves. He was very happy because he could walk to work. My son was saving his money so he could buy his own clothes and shoes. When he'd been working there for at least a year, the store went out of business. It was unexpected, but my son dealt with it. Afterward, he got heavy into his music.

There was always something going on with the kids; if you've got kids, you know. You have to keep your eyes on them at all times. My grandson was almost a year old now and one day he was sitting near a lamp in his mom's room and somehow the lamp fell over on him, and burned his fat little cheek. Poor baby, he had to be taken to the hospital, and the hospital called child protective services. They didn't know whether it was abuse or not. My oldest daughter was watching him at the time, but protective services had to investigate to see if the burn had been an accident or a case of a child being abused. People came to the house to ask my daughter lots of questions, but they found no neglect, so that was the end of that.

My son, whose hair I'd started to grow out and braid, graduated at seventeen with an advanced diploma. He received all types of certificates. He wasn't skipped or anything, but he did his schoolwork. I stayed on him. Parents, that's what we have to do. I knew my son was popular, especially with the girls, but he had to get his schoolwork done.

When he'd been gone from my house for two years, I still had Professor's son at home, eating up my food, when both young men should have graduated at the same time. I'm not saying my son was without fault, but whatever he did, he respected me enough to keep it to himself. My step -son was different. He would bring drugs, women, and whatever else he thought he could get away with into my home. When I caught him, I put him out, and took his key, because I didn't take disrespect from my own kids so I wasn't about to accept it from him.

I heard from that young man's mother again, but this time it was on the day of Professor's son's graduation. After the ceremony, she even came over to thank me for making sure he'd graduated. As little as a week before his graduation I had yet been on the case. I'd called the school to speak to a counselor. I wanted to know if he would graduate. That was when his counselor told me he was one credit short. I asked was there anything that had been missed. The counselor saw that Son had done some debates, so she said those would equal one credit. I was glad to hear that he would graduate after all! I was excited to know that my being the best [step] mom that I could have been to him hadn't been pointless. I was glad because he had to get the hell out of my house.

There were happy times too at Sequoyah. There were times of laughter, and there was the smell of fried chicken in the air. Other times there was the good smell of cakes baking in the oven and so many other wonderful things; I was cooking all the time, and the girls stayed with us until they saved enough money to get their own place.

Professor was a carpenter, so he was always out building something, but when he was home we had a good time watching TV, eating popcorn, and a lot of other fun stuff. But the girls weren't that crazy about their step-brother, and something was always going on with him and my middle daughter. Even though all the kids were working, he hadn't gotten an apartment yet. Still he knew that some of the time I carried cash, and on one particular weekend my step-son wanted me to cash his check. When my daughter found out I did, she came running down the steps cursing and screaming.

She asked how I could cash *his* check and not hers; he wasn't my damn son! I kindly told her I had no idea she'd wanted me to cash her check. I was sitting in the dining room, looking out my patio window and I could see her reflection. Behind me, she was practically standing over me, like she wanted to whip my butt. I told her, "You'd better get from over my head." Furthermore I said, "As long as you live, and I remain your mom, you'd better never curse or raise your voice at me again—or I will knock your tall slinky ass through that patio window, with the glass right behind you." From that day on, she never tried me like that again, but she did try other stuff, but I always told my kids that anything that I was confronted with, I could handle.

My middle daughter had her son in September, one month after we moved to Sequoyah. She was big as a pregnant tick carrying that baby. When she went into labor, I rode with her to the hospital by rescue squad, but there was an accident on the way, and the rescue squad stopped to attend to the wounded. While that was going on, I sat in the rescue vehicle with my daughter while she went through her labor pains. Finally we arrived at the hospital where she was in labor for another hour. Then she birthed a beautiful baby boy with a head full of hair. After all of that, I could see one tear roll out of her left eye.

My oldest daughter was working full time at an electronics store, trying to save up as much money as she could so that when the year was up, she would be ready to make her exit. My two girls shared a room together in my and Professor's house, and so did the boys. During the very beginning, when our family moved to Sequoyah, you could always expect a fight. If I didn't know any better, I would have thought we were in the Wild West, or Compton where there are gang wars at all times.

Every evening after school this one particular woman would drive a van load of her kids to a spot out back of my garage. I would hear them out there fighting other kids who lived in Sequoyah, and most of the time that mean-spirited woman's kids were the ones who had started stuff at school. She should have let her kids fight their own battles instead of her being out there, a grown woman with weave flying everywhere, getting into fights too. How would her kids learn, if their mom, a loud hot ghetto mess, was always fighting for them?

That area was a red district for drugs, and seemed like every time I turned around the cops had a group of boys lined on one side of the street. One night I was downstairs talking to my son, and I had to run upstairs to get something. Before I went up, he was lying on the couch watching TV. He'd had no shoes on, just socks. By the time I got back downstairs he had gone outside, looking for his step-brother, because he had heard police sirens. I took off outside, loudly calling him. Come to find out he was on the other side of the street with about fifteen other kids, sitting down on the curb. I told my son to come on, but the policeman told me to back up. I told that officer, "I will back up, but my son is going with me."

I had no idea my step-son was involved. I do know the cop was checking the kids for drugs. I told the policeman that my son had come outside to look for his step-brother, after he heard the sirens. Then I was able to take them inside. Policemen in that area were always trying to put all the black kids in the same category—thugs—even if they only wore a scully cap on their heads. I told the officers to their faces, "You are not going to harass my son while we live here."

I always told my son to be very careful. I always told him to make sure that everything on his car was legal. I told him that he was a young black man in America, and as such, he was subject to being pulled over at any time. It's shameful, but a lot of the time that is just the way it is. I said I didn't want him to be another statistic. I told him that throughout history black men had been lynched and thrown in ditches, many times for no reason other than they were African-American. I explained to my son why he shouldn't have a carload of young men riding around. One of them could have drugs on him and if they were pulled over, then my son would wind up going to jail too. I advised him to choose his friends wisely. I quoted Proverbs from the bible and said 'a man that walketh with a wise man shall be wise, but a companion of fools shall be destroyed.'

One night my son had been to the studio working on his music and he told me he was on his way to his friend's house, if it was alright with me. He did that because I'd always told him to call and let me know what his plans were. After I got off the phone with him, in less than five minutes, I got another call. It was my son telling me the police had pulled him over, just because he looked like the other kids in the neighborhood.

At the time he had recently received his temporary issue license, and the police took it from him. He hadn't even gotten his real card yet. I snapped. I instructed my son to go on to his friend's house. I said I would take care of things in the morning. The next day was Sunday. I went right over to the police department and demanded my son's license back. I told the officer that he'd had no right to treat my son as he had, just because my son was black. I told that officer he was racist and if he came from behind that bullet-proof glass, I would show him something. Well, he remained a racist because he never came from behind that glass. I also told him if he wasn't going to work with me, I needed his superior to call me so I could get the situation handled.

That evening the supervisor called me. He was a black man. He and I worked things out.

My son continued to go to the studio to work on his music. I wasn't willing to allow anyone to stop him, not even the police. I always told my kids, "You have to know the law, because if you don't, the police will say or do anything to you, and maybe even leave you for dead." I explained, "In case you don't know, some officers have a code where they will lie and cover up for one another." I'm not saying they're all bad, but some of them are. In spite of that I planned to stand up for my kids, because black youngsters were a hot topic in that area because there was a gang there, and because of those red districts for drugs.

Other than going to the studio, my son loved to go skating on Friday nights. On this particular night, I didn't go. I had turned in early. The next morning he told me that the police from Maryland had been chasing him on the Belt-way. Nahum told me that prior to the chase, he had been getting off at his exit and some car started to chase him because the other driver felt my son had cut him off. When the police caught up with my son, they said he was driving recklessly. They also called for backup that included about eight police cruisers—for one black man. Thank God I always pray for my children before I go to bed, and that night was no different. After my son told them what happened, they gave him a ticket.

While they were growing up, I always told my children not to be afraid of the police, even though there were corrupt ones. "But," I said, "they are just people, they use the bathroom just like we do." I advised my children never to smart-mouth an officer, simply out of respect, because that officer could say my child did something totally different and then leave them somewhere dead. Mothers, you have to always make sure you teach your children as much as you can about the law, so when they face this corrupt world alone, they will know how to handle themselves.

When my son was in high school, the gang of that neighborhood was determined to hurt my son, as I stated before. So I took him out of the school that he was in and put him in a school where I was teaching at the time. After my son graduated, about two years later, he decided he wanted his own place. That was okay with me because I had been praying for about two years so I would be ready. I remember that my son told me he wanted to move and be on his own because he wanted to see what the world had to offer. He said if he failed he would just get back up and try again.

I was more than confident that my son would be alright. Anything Nahum asked to do, if I said no, he would wait until I gave him permission to do it. I will give you an example; this is the tattoo incident. Now remember, most American parents will usually tell their child wait until you are grown, or eighteen to get a tattoo, but that's not a law. My son was a good kid and since I'd said to, he'd waited. I will never forget his eighteenth birthday though.

That morning he came in my room and said, "Ma, I am eighteen today and I am going to get my tattoo." What could I say? I just looked at him and smiled. Not only was he a hard worker, he was going to use his own money to do it.

I told you earlier, I have two daughters and one son. While they were in school we would go shopping together, to buy clothes and shoes. I remember…the kids would never disrespect me about things. Well let me take that back, my middle daughter had a lot of mouth, so she would speak her mind, but she wasn't disrespectful. Anyhow, many times I took my kids to the pay less for shoes store, so right after my son graduated from high school he was working two jobs and taking very good care of himself. He even bought a pair of one hundred and fifty dollar sneakers.

When he got home, he tried them on again so I could see them. Then he looked at me and looked at his shoes and said, "I'm not paying all this money for no shoes…" He told me, "Now I know what you mean." My son took those shoes back and bought three good pairs and still had money left.

He is something else, even now, he is very particular when it comes to his money, and that's a good thing. Just because he was working two jobs back then, he still knew his limits when it came to his money. He was disciplined from an early age. Due to his father's death, he grew up faster than he would have otherwise. And even though there were gangs in the area where we lived, that fact taught my son to be tough and stand up for himself.

15 / THE CAR DILEMMA

As long as I can remember, my son has always had an old soul. He always thinking years ahead, about what he would do in certain situations and about what he would do with his life. Ever since he was six, he was like a little old man. At that age he said he wanted to be an airplane pilot, until he found it was a lot of work. Then he changed his mind. He said, "I don't want to do that."

I felt he was mature for his age. As a mom I was determined to teach all my children things they would need to know about life. I put each one through driving school when I felt they were ready. Before I officially allowed my son to go, I taught him the rules of the road myself so he would be prepared when he got behind the wheel with an instructor.

He got his license at fifteen years and eight months old because at that time he could obtain it then. Yet before he was officially labeled a driver, we had to go to a ceremony where when your child's name was called you could say whether or not you felt he was ready for the road. When they called my son's name I stood up and said, "Oh no, I don't think he's ready." Nahum jerked around and couldn't believe it. Seeing the serious look on my face, he had no idea I was joking. I then told the man, "Aw he's okay," and my son was able to walk up and receive his license.

I told him if he got any speeding tickets I would ground him. He got a speeding ticket the first week! Then he called himself hiding it from me. Every day, he kept asking if he got any mail. Well, one day he explained that he was expecting mail from the courts. I looked at him and asked, "You expecting mail this quick?" He got quiet, knowing that I could tell when he was lying. I went to get his mail and asked, "You're looking for this?" He opened it, and since it was a speeding ticket, I had to stick to my word. I grounded him; I gave him one week, to teach him a lesson. Actually, he didn't say a word, he just handed me his keys and went away sad with his head and shoulders bowed. I'll never forget that day. He is a good son.

With my approval, my son bought his first car when he was sixteen and that's when all the wolves came out.

 Some kids were angry because he had a car, because he was good-looking, because he could sing, and because he had the attention of quite a few girls. Seeing this, I told my son, "You have to be careful, because girls and women like to keep stuff going." I told him it would be stuff like telling their boyfriends that he was flirting with them so a fight could break out. I told Nahum "Concentrate on your grades and worry about the girls later."

When he was sixteen, my son bought a Mercury Sable, the outside was nice, but the engine was a mess. He wasn't by himself though when he got it. He and I went together, and we were sold the biggest lemon on the lot. That car would always break down somewhere, night or day. My son could be at the studio and he'd call and I would have to have it towed home. Back then I didn't know about the three day lemon law, but I'm sure the salesman did. I was so upset with that raggedy car dealership and I was even more upset that we had been sold a lemon. I was really ready to tear that salesman and that car lot up.

One day someone hit my son. He didn't get hurt or anything and I had insurance. The other driver was at fault. The only thing was…it was a hit and run. My son came home and showed me where his car had been hit. I called my insurance company and told them of the incident. My son was able to get a big fat check. Right after that I called the lender and told them to pick up that raggedy car before I drove it into the Potomac River. They knew I was serious and they picked it up the next day.

Now I will tell you about my son's first brand new car. I will never forget the day he came in from work, and said, "Mom, I want you and Yolanda to go down with me to the car dealership so I can show you the car I will buy." He told me he didn't need my help, he just wanted me and his sister to see his brand new car. I have never been more proud of my son than I was that day. He was stepping out on his own, doing things without me.

While my kids were growing up I told them that no matter what they wanted in life, they had to persevere until they reached their goal. Well, we arrived at the dealership as the salesman was just finishing up the paperwork. My son showed me and his sister his new car. He said, "Mom while he is finishing the papers I will walk around my car seven times." I looked at Nahum in amazement and said while bobbing my head, "Since you are walking around it, you might as well make it eight times, for a new beginning." You see, whatever you instill in your kids, they will remember. My son and his sisters always heard me talking about seven being the number of completion, so he took it upon himself to see if it would work for him. He was able to drive his car off the lot that day, a Dodge Neon. He was so happy he could finally afford a car that wasn't going to leave him stranded.

After a few days, he got a letter telling him his loan wasn't approved. My son wasn't concerned in the least, because he had walked around his car and he wasn't about to hear anything else. Everything worked out. Things were going fine for him; he had a good job, was paying his car note every month, and he was going to the studio where he worked on his music. He was the happiest camper I had seen in a long time.

Still, there came a day when I felt uneasy concerning my son. When that happens, I don't second guess, I do what

I know best to do, and that is pray. About four a.m. the next morning I felt the urge to go outside and walk around Nahum's car seven times, on the eighth time I sat in it and prayed. I gladly followed that unction. Then about a week later, early one morning I got a call from my son's friend saying that Nahum's car had been totaled. I wasn't worried, because my mind quickly raced back to the early morning when I'd walked around his new car. I believe because I followed the voice of the Lord his life was spared. The car was done, but the only thing my son had to show that he had been in an accident was a little scar by his music tattoo, on his hand. You can still see it today.

My son was a little devastated for a while because he loved that car, and it suited him, but I told him, "You can get many more cars, but not another life." Since that time, he has indeed bought and paid for many cars, just like I said. He had a car prior to the Sable, and that car didn't make any sense because sometimes it wouldn't start with the key, but he would touch something under the hood and get it going. I think I allowed him to keep that one for about four months, but from day one it was nothing but trouble. I said, "Until I get you another car, just use Pat and Turner." He asked, "What's that?" My reply was, "Pat your feet and turn the corner."

16 / WILLIAMS HIGH

My nine siblings and I graduated from T.C. Williams High School. My son would make the eleventh person from the same family tree to do so. However, my siblings and I had gone to T.C. by choice, but my son went due to force. People at the school that he'd previously attended made it hard for him to have a good year. Because my son was popular with the girls, there was always some drama going on, even though he wasn't serious about anyone at the time. The around-the-way thugs were already jealous of him because he was light-skinned and had nice braids, but the real trouble started when he got a set of wheels.

It was my son's last year in school, and I wasn't about to put up with any drama. I knew he was already having a hard time dealing with his father's death, but he would never talk about it. He didn't need any more trouble, and especially none from the jealous thugs who were members of a neighborhood gang. They were always going from place to place, starting fights. So I told my son not to allow people to ride in his car because they might put drugs in there, then if he was pulled over, the cops would charge *him* because it was his car.

He listened, and most of the time he rode by himself; then the thugs thought he was trying to be better than them. My son just couldn't seem to do anything right, not where they were concerned. Transferring my son to T.C. Williams High School proved easy because at the time I worked there and I wanted his last year to be full of joy and peace. After the transfer, Nahum was ok, for a while…until someone tried to take his car when he went to lunch at McDonalds.

A misguided young man that didn't even attend the school attempted to carjack my son. Remember now, I was teaching at that school, so my son appeared at my classroom door to tell me that it had been during lunch that this incident had taken place. I looked at Nahum and told him not to worry. I said I would look into it, but I'm telling you, I'd thought we'd left all the thugs at the prior high school. Still, to protect my son I didn't care what I had to, as long as it was legal, and as long as it didn't involve transferring him again.

I reported the incident to the campus police because the carjacker, had to be stopped, but that criminal kept bringing new gang members up to the school—to fight my son. I told you about it. Once I even heard him and others in the parking lot cussing and talking about how they were going to get that nigger Nate. They were using terrible language. Since Criminal didn't know me, I simply got in my van and went and reported his troublesome self to the campus police. He was arrested that same day, right in front of me. He was taken away. But…he came back, after he got out of jail…

Another thing that happened before the carjack incident was a coach from school appointed him self my son's manager. Nahum ran home after school and said he had joined a group and a coach from school was his manager. That coach had heard my son singing one of Sam Cooke's songs, and all that coach could see was dollar signs, but I wanted more details before I jumped on the coach, even though he had no right to do what he did without my consent. I have told many parents that everyone who smiles at their child doesn't always mean them well.

I was very upset when I told my son that the group wasn't going to happen right then. I said when he finished school I would help him get started. I said "If anyone is going to manage you, it will be me." He went back to school the next day and told the coach what I said, but that man was determined to go over my head! He even called my house and asked to speak to my son. I didn't allow that. I told the coach not to ever call my house again, and not to try and persuade my son to allow him to be his manager.

Mothers, when you have young children, especially boys, you must make sure you don't allow them to be eaten by wolves. I'm telling you, I have been through many things with my son. Mothers, you need to know that if your child has a destiny, many things will come against them, and you, but you have to be strong. You've got to pray and face things head on.

I will never forget the cold night in October of 1998 when about sixty boys from a neighborhood gang showed up at my house, to hurt my son. I mentioned this before, but fate had it that I was home that evening, I hadn't gone to my usual poetry reading at a local chain book store. Looking back, I know that if I had not been home that night there would have been a bloodbath. The sad thing was the police never showed up when I called. They knew it was the same thugs, those in the neighborhood gang, but the cops stayed away because everybody involved was black. I understand. That's what they do sometimes, but my son wasn't a thug or a gang member. I realize too that the police didn't care that it would have wound up black on black crime. Yet I thank God those thugs finally left my house...

What happened was on this particular cold evening, I went out to the trash can to get rid of something. When I turned around to go back in the house, just that quick, not only had all these thugs arrived, but my son was outside too, in a fighting stance. I called out to those thugs that I was not going to let all of them jump on my son or his brother. I said in a loud voice, "If I allowed them [my sons] to fight you all, one on one, my boys would beat y'all all over this complex."

There was one particular young man who stepped up, like he was going to fight my son. Don't forget now, these thugs had known it was my night to be out. They knew my schedule—because of my son's best friend. He had a big mouth. Also, they hadn't seen my car, but I 'd been led to park it elsewhere, earlier in the evening. So since I was at home, I asked the young man who'd appointed himself 'the fighter' what was his name. He told me, but my sixteen year old son called out, "Your name ain't no damn Johnny," or whatever name the young man said.

By that time, I used my cordless to call the police, again. I told my son to go in the house, him and his step-brother. At the time I thought my step-son was obeying me. I was unaware that he had run into the house to get my husband's sawed off shotgun—the one that I hadn't even known was there! Mind you now, my son was still outside, by the door and I was trying to get him inside. That was when I heard the click of the shotgun behind me. In all that confusion, I turned around and ordered my step-son to give me the gun.

He didn't want to, and tempers were flying high. "No, Ma. No," my step-son said. "I'm tired of them all the time trying to mess with my brother."

I finally got the loaded gun from my second son, but inside the house, my son was so angry until he used his fist to put a hole in the wall. I couldn't sit still, so I paced back 'n forth, crying and holding that gun. Then I heard my son calmly say, "Ma, give me the gun."

"No," I told him.

Again, my son said, "Ma, give me the gun."

I said no again, while I kept pacing back and forth.

Then my son said, "Ma...dad taught me how to load and unload a gun when he took me deer hunting."

I realized that had to have been when Nahum had been about eight years old. Confident that he would do what was right, I gave him the gun. He unloaded it and gave me the shells. I put the shotgun up on a shelf. Then I went back outside, while my boys were inside, and all I could see were gang members. Most of them were taller and bigger than me. They were milling around in the parking lot so I walked out among them and as I did I asked a question. I wanted to know where two specific young men were. I called to them. I asked them to step out of the crowd. No one moved, and no one looked me in the eye.

I spotted a young man who was supposed to have been my son's friend. I pulled him from the crowd and quoted Proverbs 13:20, "*He that walketh with wise men shall be wise, but a companion of fools shall be destroyed.*" Then I shook my finger as I sternly said, "Keep walking with fools!" I meant it as a warning. Then I turned and went back inside.

Strangely enough, I hadn't even been afraid while I was out there. The Lord was with me. Although so many things happened that night, and even though that was an ordeal, I am glad it ended peacefully.

I was glad to get my son to a new school too, where he would make new friends. It was bad enough that he'd often had to deal with jealous peers, but when he wound up having to put up with garbage from teachers, it was a bit much. You see I had to pull him completely out of the class of a male teacher who was racist. Then I had to tell a totally different teacher that if she didn't leave my son alone, I would have to teach her class myself. That happened to be my son's drama class and he wanted to be there, but the teacher made things hard for him. I informed the woman teacher that if she couldn't stand my son being happy every day, then she didn't need to teach drama.

While he was in that high school, I told my son that I was getting ready to start the first step team there. I asked if he wanted to be the president. I did so because I wanted to keep him busy in his spare time, so that I could keep him out of trouble and so he could be at peace.

Nahum told his friends what I was about to do. He also asked if they wanted to be part of the team. They all wanted to step, so we made my son the official president and we started practicing every evening, at the school. We were preparing for a half-time show, and shows at other high schools. We had a total of eight boys and thirteen girls. For that step team, my son made up so many routines, and we went to countless shows all over the area. By this time my son already knew he would become a singer, and so did other people. That was part of why the haters came out, seemingly from everywhere.

While he was in T.C., the high school, my son started a group and called it TAKIR, which stood for Talented and Keeping It Real. The group was made up of four friends who practiced hard every day to prepare themselves for any type of show, and every talent show they entered, they did so to win. My son was the leader of the group and they traveled all over the Washington D.C., Maryland, and Virginia area where they became well known. Even with all of this, I never would have dreamed that my son would one day become a household name.

By this time, we'd made it to the halfway point in Nahum's senior year and things were going well. He and the senior class were making preparations to go on the college tour which took place every year. He was very excited because his choice colleges were Clark-Atlanta and Morehouse. Both are in Georgia, but for me, it didn't matter where he went; I simply had to give him a refresher course on how he was to carry himself while he was away.

Leaving for the tour, the charter buses were set to take off early. Everyone was enthusiastic—probably more so about getting away from school for a few days. I told my son to call me when they arrived in Atlanta. He did and I experienced excitement too because he would be my last child to attend college. However, before the trip I told him, "Don't let anybody call me for anything stupid." My son's reply was that he wouldn't. It wasn't like I often got phone calls about my son's behavior, but some of the teachers lumped every senior in the same category—that of clowns.

About a day into the trip, not only did I get a phone call, I received it at four a.m. Morning calls like that are never good, but I picked up the phone. The male voice on the other end had the nerve to say that he was sorry to disturb me at that time of morning, but a complaint was received that 'they' were making too much noise in my son's room. I told Mr. Scary, a teacher who worked alongside me at T.C., the male teacher who'd gone on the senior trip, that if he couldn't handle a little noise, then he should have stayed home. I told him to let the kids enjoy themselves. I also said, "Don't call me again about anything stupid." Then I told him to let me speak to my son. When Nahum got on the phone, I told him if he was making noise, to calm it down some. I said, "Get through this trip without incident." I have always felt that there are a few teachers who have book knowledge, but no social skills, and the way that man was acting, you'd have thought my son had robbed somebody or something worse. A few days later, when I saw the male teacher who'd called me, I told him he was one of those teachers who couldn't function outside a classroom, and boy did I hit a nerve!

You may have heard the myth that women can't raise men. Well that's all it is; a myth, because my son turned out fine, and look where he is today. Admittedly, back when my husband died, all of a sudden, I'd had no time to prepare for how I was going to raise our son. Still, I knew that as long as I had my God, a few dependable supporters, and prayer, my son was not going to become another African-American statistic. He was not going to wind up stuck in a jail cell, nor would he wind up strung out on drugs. Why? Because every day I told my son I loved him. I made sure he knew that if he needed me, I would be there, no matter what.

Well, despite all the trials and tribulations that he and I faced, my son graduated from my old high school. After graduation, he enrolled in Clark-Atlanta University, with plans to become an engineer, or he would major in music. But right after enrollment he decided he would work on his music for a year and see where it would take him. I gave the ok, and one year turned into two. When things didn't work out with the first group, my son started another group that he called 295, after a beltway. He worked real hard with that group. They went to record labels all over New York and Los Angeles, but nobody wanted to deal with groups at the time.

 I told my son that when the rubber meets the road, he would have to make a decision about the group thing. When he finally faced that the group wouldn't go anywhere, Nahum told me that he'd decided to go solo. Then as soon as he went solo, record labels wanted him! Later he would even find out, from his manager, after he auditioned for Capitol Records, that the labels had wanted him all along.

When Nahum told the group he was going solo, as you can imagine, they were not pleased. Still, he said, "I've got to do this for myself," and he has been going forward ever since. I have to tell you though, that my son has a kind heart, because he really didn't want to leave the group behind.

When they were knee-high to a duck—as the old folks often say, I taught my kids how to be responsible. I told them that I sent them to school to learn, not to be the class clowns. I did that because I think ninety-nine percent of the time it's up to parents how their kids turn out. The way kids end up usually all goes back to their upbringing.

My kids knew I said what I meant, and meant what I said. So they knew I wasn't playing when I told them they'd better not lose one school book. If they had lost them, then I would have had to pay the school so that the school could replace the book for the next student coming on. Even when he was in the first grade, I told my son there would be no losing books. I told all my kids I didn't care what they had to do; they had to keep their books in good shape. I said so because when the end of the school year rolled around, I didn't want to pay one dime for books. I remember all of this like it happened yesterday.

I even remember that nearing his high school graduation, my son went to pick up his robe and was told that not only would he not get his robe, he couldn't walk on graduation day! The school staff said so because they believed he owed for books. I knew that was untrue, because at the end of every year my son didn't owe the school one penny. What's more is I had even paid the money that other kids rightfully owed for books that they'd mislaid or destroyed. So I told my son not to worry, he had other things to deal with. I said, "I got this," because if I had any say, he was going to walk down that aisle! After all he had been through to graduate, I was not about to let him be robbed of that joy or that experience.

Little did he know, but I was getting ready to tear that school up, so to speak, if somebody didn't come up with the right answer for me. One thing everybody knew; from the students, to the teachers, to the janitor; was that I was not to be played with. I was to be reckoned with. When I knew my kids were wrong, I dealt with them, so the same went for others. I dealt with anyone or anything that came down the pipe.

Understand something. With me it wasn't always about my children. I helped many other people's children. Still, it upset me to see what appeared to be a thousand books jammed in lockers on the last day of school, because either the kids or their parents hadn't cared enough to take care of or return those books. Then they wound up paying for them, but I was different. I could think of better things to do with my money.

To get out of high school, my son went through struggles and tackled obstacles. Many times he wanted to give up, but I told him, "You are not giving up. You have to persevere. Giving up is not an option." I said so because what if as soon as he threw in the towel, his destiny was right around the corner?

Sure, I was trying to make it, and still trying hard myself to deal with my husband's death. Sometimes I didn't feel like getting out of bed, but I had to because there was no one else to make sure that my son was kept on the right path. My children never knew the devastation I dealt with, for years. I even have my moments now, but I had to keep my head above water. As a mother, I had to make sure my son was going to make it.

17 / AFTER GRADUATION

After graduation my son got two jobs so he could save enough money to get his first apartment. I wasn't worried about him because he was mature enough to be on his own. He was still singing with the group, and they were doing ok, but nothing looked like it was leading to a record deal. Yet my son decided to stick with the group for a while and see where it would take him. While he saved his money, he was still living at home and that was ok because he was doing something positive. I was worried about him driving so much, because some cops had problems with black kids, especially if they were driving, and my son was always coming home from the studio late at night or in the wee hours of the morning.

One night he called and said he was going to stay at a friend's until morning, since it was already late. I told him to go ahead. I said, "Just call me when you get there."

When my son got to his friend's house he called and told me that a cop had pulled him over and took his license. It seemed that officer had an attitude because my son had a car. I told my son it would be ok, that I would look into the next day which was Sunday.

Early that morning before I went to church I went right over to the station. I told the receptionist that I was looking for Officer Butt. When I received a quizzical reply and stare, I said that must have been the man's name because that's what he'd been acting like. Confronted by the officer, I told him who I was and why I was there. I made sure he knew who my son was because I wanted to hear what that man had to say.

Well, after he finished lying on my son I told him to step from behind the glass that separated us. I announced, "I will give you something to talk about." I said so because those policemen in the county where I lived were bullying many of the black kids and their parents. That was the reason I looked that officer right in his face and told him, "You are not going to harass my son just because he is black." I also added, "By the way, my son is not a thug."

I let that officer know that I wanted him to give me what he had taken from my son. I said, "If you choose not to, then I need to talk to your superior."

Later on that day the superior officer called me. During our conversation, he had the nerve to say, "Well, I've never had any complaints involving that officer." I did not fail to state that things happen. Then being wicked, he pushed me to say, "Either you clear up this problem, or I will sue the entire police department." I said so and meant it because I had always been told that either you stand for something or you will fall for anything.

During the time that my son was singing with the group, I could tell when he would become discouraged. I would always remind him that God had placed good people in his life to work with him. When he finally obtained the right team, he felt things were moving right along. I explained to him that if it got to the point that nothing was happening with the group then he would have to cut his loses and keep moving.

He let me know he had a time limit on everything. When that time came, and nothing had happened he said, he would go solo. I had no reason to doubt him because he knew when enough was enough. Sometimes though, people feel if they change the name of a group that will solve the problem. It didn't, but the group traveled from city to city, state to state, and they sat before multiple record label executives, all to no avail.

The group finally split up in the summer. Then all kinds of opportunities began to manifest for my son. I was so happy because whenever he was burdened down, so was I.

He would later tell me that no one had been interested in group, but that they'd wanted him as a solo artist. My young man thought he was telling me something new, but

I already knew the layout. I had just been waiting for things to come full circle.

Nahum couldn't hide the smallest detail from me. I always knew when things weren't going right, and when they were. During very difficult times in his career, he would tell me he wanted to give up. Those times I would remind him of what God had spoken in October of 2000. My son had been promised fame, fortune, and travel. I admitted I didn't know what else was going on; I said I didn't know who else wasn't getting a contract, "but," I said, "*You* will get one."

If I wasn't calling, I was texting, and I would've sent a note on a piece of paper if I thought it would reach my son. I encouraged him so much until he finally got it in his mind. I think he began to feel like: if mom believes, I will too, because I know her faith in God.

He had gotten so anxious, he said mom I think I'll try out for American Idol. I said, "I pray that you get a contract before the show rolls around again." I said so because I didn't want to deal with Simon, because it would not have been a pretty scene.

My son called me one day and said he had something in the works, but he had to wait a week to go to L.A. I told him that when the time was right he would go, and that he would get a contract. I was sure of that. And wouldn't you know? One week later he was calling me from L.A. yelling on the phone. He told me he had just auditioned in front of the executives of Capitol Records. He sang four songs, three of which he wrote, and got a contract on the spot! That day was joyous for the both of us.

Since my son had such a time dealing with his dad's death, he decided to allow those feelings to pour out on his first album. I had flown out to Los Angeles maybe three months after he was signed to Capital records. He wasn't well known at the time, but he was on his way. I always told my children as they were growing up, never look down on anybody. I said it because they didn't know; they just may have been talking to the next billionaire. I wanted them never to think they were better than the next person. I taught my kids if they had half a penny to still keep their chins up, because the sun would one day shine on them.

During my stay in Los Angeles and Hollywood, my girl-friend and I enjoyed ourselves. It wasn't like I was running up and down Hollywood Boulevard, but I was happy that my son had obtained a contract with one of the biggest record labels.

Now one day I walked up to the label building and asked the young security man if my friend and I could go in and sightsee and take a few pictures. He looked down at me and sarcastically said, "Miss, they don't do that anymore—not unless you know someone here."

I gave him a long stern look, and told him not to worry about it, because my son would take me inside the very next day. As soon as that young man realized that I wasn't just some woman going to the beach, he wanted to know who my son was.

I replied, "A minute ago I was nobody—to you, so don't worry about who my son is."

I winked at my girlfriend, gave that hired fellow the talk-to-the-hand sign and told her to snap the picture. I could have made things bad for him that day, but I had bigger fish to fry. But really, people need to get a grip and stop thinking they are better that other people.

When my son arrived the next day, he wanted to know if I wanted to go to the label, because he wanted to see the man that had disrespected his mom. I am glad my son doesn't take mess off people. I taught him to always stand up for himself.

While I was at his hotel, I was inquiring about his managers and he told me he'd put them out of his room. They had been trying to make him do another song, yet they hadn't paid him for the one he'd already finished for someone else. Listen, you may have people over you, or helping you, but that does not mean you have to be a pushover.

After his first album was released, I had to do a little undercover work. I wanted to see who was bootlegging his album. On the streets, as soon as I discovered someone with my son's name on their illegal CD list, I would tell them that either they had to take his name off their list or I would turn them in to Bad Beat, a company where anyone can report people who sell bootleg items. I had the number in my phone. Anyway, I didn't trust that those hustlers would do the right thing so I turned them in. I even turned a few barbers in. Them being good with hair had nothing to do with them illegally making money by bootlegging my son's album. I told people that was exactly why my son's album hadn't gone platinum at the time.

I told him what I had done; teasing me he said, "Mom you are crazy." However, one thing my kids know about me is I can handle anything that comes down the pipe. I have even told bootleggers to get a real job, and this was way before the economy went belly-up. I told those street hustlers that my son had many sleepless nights trying to get to where he is, "And all you can do is bootleg his album."

I told some of my own family members that if they didn't stop bootlegging, I would turn them into too. I said it didn't have anything to do with family, it was just business. As a parent you have to stick with your kids, through the storm and the rain. You cannot allow them to give up. Tell them there will be no throwing in the towel. That is not an option.

I say that because my son went through so many dark days after his father died so suddenly, not giving anybody any warning that he was sick. If my husband's death devastated me, what do you think it did to an eleven year old little boy? Thank god I was a level-headed mom, because if I hadn't been, I don't know what would have happened to my boy. By the help of God we made it through, but we had to face many sleepless nights and dreadful days.

Mothers, I know this may be the case for some of you, but please allow your kids to be what they want to be, if it's positive. Don't try and force them to go to college, just because you only had a third grade education. Always remember, your kids aren't you, and you have to allow them to follow their dreams. Not once have I regretted that my son wanted to work on his music for one year. I know that if I hadn't allowed him to follow his dreams I would have many regrets, and so would he. Kids are dropping out of schools and colleges by the millions because some parents are pushing too hard. All we can do as parents is support our kids and make sure they stay focused.

As long as my children didn't want to make a career out of selling, doings drugs, or any other type of criminal activity, I was good. If that's the case with your kids, you should be too. If your son or daughter wants to be a street sweeper, tell them not to leave one piece of trash on anybody's street. Tell them to simply do their best, whatever they choose to do. Isn't that what the late great Dr. Martin Luther King, Jr. said?

18 / THE SHOE REMEDY

Shoes are one of the biggest things in any kid's life, whether that kid is from the suburbs or the ghetto. Knowing this didn't mean a thing to me, because my kids were not going to grow up thinking they had to get every brand name shoe or sneaker that hit the market. In life, I wanted my kids to know quality versus quantity.

While growing up, my son always wanted brand name shoes. I could have gotten him some from time to time, but I never wanted to do what everybody else was doing, I wanted to be different. That was why I told him and his sisters that I would buy them *one* brand name pair of shoes per year. The rest of the time they knew. We were going to the pay less for shoes store. I also said, "If you get an attitude about it, I will take you to the thrift store." You know they didn't want that, but there are some nice things in the thrift store.

Some parents just let their kids tell them what to do and what not to do. I didn't. I told my kids that when they got old enough to get a job then they could buy their own shoes. They could buy a house, a car, and anything else they wanted because they would be using their own money. I always saw parents giving kids everything they wanted as a problem because as far as I could see, the parents were setting the kids up for a fall. The reason I say that is simple, if you are always buying your kids the most expensive shoes, they will feel that is the way of life. Then they will get an attitude when or if they can't get those things.

I grew up in poverty so it would seem like I'd have wanted to get my kids expensive things, but to me that was never the answer. I believe parents have to teach their children values, because if you fail to do so, both you and they may regret it, later. I'm going to tell you…I see so many kids raising their parents, and lately it seems to have gotten worse. There used to be a time when black parents wouldn't allow that, but now they're jumping on the bandwagon too. It's not good. Mothers and fathers, if you allow your children to tell you what to do, then you will end up with all types of problems with them, and they'll end up with all kinds of problems in the world.

As soon as my son got old enough to work and buy his own things, the first thing he did was buy a pair of shoes that cost one hundred and fifty dollars. He brought them home, looked at them on his feet and said, "These shoes aren't all that." My young man took those shoes back and got three good pairs for the price of one.

What I have always tried to explain to parents is that kids have no idea what a brand name is. It is the parents who start training the child as soon as they are old enough to understand. Parents help make consumers of their kids. Then they find they can't keep up with the child's wants as well as his needs; when it is the job of the parent to train the child in the way they should go as soon as he or she can understand.

Speaking of training, I had a specific saying that my kids will probably never forget, it was "If you ever raise your hand to hit me, there will only be two hits. I will hit you, and you will hit the floor." I also told them, "When you get too tall for me to reach, I will stand on a chair and hit you." Some parents get a little ridiculous though, saying things like 'I brought you in this world and I will take you out.' Now that is a threat all day long.

When I took my kids shopping, they already knew, before we entered the store, what the deal was. There would be no hard feelings regarding our shopping experience, or just because I only bought them one pair of brand name shoes per year. They knew that didn't mean I loved them less, it simply meant I had more money for other things, like taking them places. I never had a problem with my kids getting into fights about the type of shoes or clothes they wore to school either, because they weren't wearing expensive items; they weren't going to a fashion show. They were going to school—to learn! My kids were simply always clean and their clothes were pressed. I feel those things showed a lot of love on my part.

When I was teaching school, sometimes I would hear Child A tell Child B that Child B had worn his clothing two days in a row. That wasn't right. However, I didn't fault Child A for the mean things he said, because he'd obviously heard similar things from some adult. I would pull Child A aside though, and have a talk with him. I'd explain that some kids don't have as much as others, so they should not be made fun of. I did that because it isn't always the kid's fault when he or she does wrong. Many times you can trace a child's behavior back to his home training. The bible says charity begins at home, and spreads abroad. So parents when you send your child to school or wherever, make sure you have taught them well.

Since I happen to be speaking of parents and children, I'd like to say this. Parents, if you allow your offspring to disrespect you, they will do other adults the same way. I never could understand why parents would allow their kids to curse in front of them, or why they would curse their children out also.

I always tried to be a good role model for my children, and believe me, sometimes it was hard, but I wanted them to be proud of me being their mom. Parents, when you let your kids do and say anything, then they will embarrass you in public. When they do, don't act like that is the first time that's happened. No one looking on will believe it. The only thing onlookers will think is that *at home* you fell down on the job—you were slacking.

My kids realized, as soon as they could say 'Mama,' that I wasn't to be played with. They weren't afraid of me, because I was loving and kind, not battering and brutal, but they respected me, because there is a big difference between the two. All I had to do was look at them and they knew what time it was.

Personally, I also have problem with parents being dressed to kill...their hair is done too, nails are done, and the kids look like they've come straight out of a shelter. If you're a parent who does this, realize one thing. Your children are a reflection of you. Don't allow them to walk around looking like no one loves them.

19 / MOVING TO ATLANTA

 When my son told me he was moving to Atlanta, I thought it would be great, for him. However, I did not say it was a great heartbreak for me. I kept quiet because I wanted him to continue to walk out his destiny. I knew he was mature enough to be on his own… but as his mother, I was concerned about him being okay.

I never let Nahum know the way I really felt because he would have worried. Yet if he had looked closely at my face he would have seen the pain, but I'm strong in all things, and I taught all my kids to have backbone too. I knew that with my son I had raised a man, not a mouse. If I didn't know any better and believe in the reincarnation of a person, I would say he had already been here before because he has such an old soul. Therefore, I knew he would do okay in Atlanta.

When he was twenty years old he was more than ready for a change. There wasn't a lot happening in the D.C. area, not pertaining to his career. He had already been working for about two years, so he needed to move on. He had been working a couple of jobs, and going to the studio at night, until the wee hours of the morning.

A lot of times I would worry about him because he had so many people who hated him without cause. So I was sort of relieved when he told me that he and the singing group he was in were moving south. His manager said he knew people in Atlanta with whom my son and the group could stay for a while. I had plenty of family there too; just in case Nahum needed anything, so I was never worried about whether or not he would be successful. He and I already knew where he was headed. My son also knew that if I had any say, I would not allow him to fail, because failure was not an option.

But I couldn't keep him from going through struggles with his group members. Thank God there were no jealous rivalries, even though he was the leader of the group. He and the other guys got along quite well. But my son had problems with the man that helped them get to Atlanta. Nahum even called me to discuss what was going on, and you know I wanted to know. He told me about one particular man. Upset, my son said he wanted to knock him out. So I told him, "Listen, you've got a destiny. You're on your way—you and the group. Y'all are trying to get a contract, so don't do anything stupid." I said, "Do not do anything you'll regret."

I couldn't step into the situation that had developed with that particular manager whom my son felt wasn't doing all he could, but things got so bad until I wound up calling my sister that lived in Georgia. I explained how things weren't going well, and that her nephew needed a break— before he hurt somebody. That was why my son moved away from where the manager had the group staying and into his aunt's house. That way everybody would get into less conflicts. Nahum stayed at my sister's house for a while, but when things finally picked up, when the group got more gigs, he was able to move into his own place. What a relief that was for me.

My son began to settle in his place, while working on his music. Still trying to make things happen, he finally decided to let the group go. He had to go solo. When he did, things began looking up. The group wasn't happy about it, but it was no surprise because from time to time in the past I'd told my son that he didn't belong in a group. I knew he was meant to be a solo artist.

I had no idea *when* he would go solo, but I knew in my heart he would. I never harassed him about the two different groups that he was part of. From time to time however,

I would ask how things were going. As a result he would always say, "Mom when I've gone as far I can—with the group, I know what to do." He always told me he wanted the group experience.

I offered my son a hypothetical situation. "What if someone presented you with a contract, but what if they didn't want the group…what if they only wanted you? What would you do?" His answer was that he would leave and go for himself. He even admitted that because he had gotten so close to the group members it would be hard to let go, but he was aware that one day he would have to.

Now when my son had initially arrived in Georgia, his first friend was a young woman he met at a club. I'll call Peaches. An attractive young lady, Peaches looked out for my son. They were good friends. Then some years later, they became romantically involved. Still, it didn't work out as well as he hoped—because of a few things. You know he was busy getting his career off the ground, and she was busy too, doing her thing.

Sometimes I would call and my son would sound so sad, down there in the south. I could tell he was very frustrated that the group hadn't gotten a deal yet. I already knew they wouldn't, ever, but I kept my mouth shut. Sometimes it is best to keep quiet, even if you know you're right. As the old saying goes 'I didn't want to rain on the group members' parade.'

However, I didn't fail to mention that maybe my son had to start thinking about doing his own thing. That was when he said to me, very plainly again, "Ma, I like the group experience, but when I've gone as far as I can with them, I'll go solo." He had a certain length of time mapped out, and if things didn't happen within that time frame, he was done. He would go it alone.

While waiting for his big break, Nahum had a lot of hardships; sometimes he wasn't eating, or sleeping. But as the saying goes, 'a mother always knows when her child is in trouble.' He might be the quiet type; he's never wanted to make much fuss about anything. Still, if things got bad enough, he would call me and all I would say was, "I wanted to see how long it was going to take you," to call me.

Finally, he got over the group thing, branched out, and moved on. Then the music industry wheels began to turn for him and he has been steadily climbing ever since.

20 / BECOMING *J. HOLIDAY*

Nahum had been doing the group thing for a few years. And as his mother I already knew that the first group, nor the second, would go anywhere. The first group was ok, and they participated in a number of talent shows and won, but the truth is...it wasn't meant for my son to be in a group.

While he still lived in the D.C. area I sat him down and told him about a dream I'd had. Even today, he knows when I tell him something I've dreamed, it will come to pass. Yet, despite the information I gave him he still wanted the group thing. He parted with the first group and formed another, but the thing was...he always stood out  from the rest of the group. It was like he was different.

After the second group moved to Atlanta, a little time passed and things weren't going well, but that was something I had already anticipated. I remember having a conversation with my son on the phone about the group and he plainly reminded me of his time limit. He said, "If nothing happens within that time, I know what I have to do." After he told me that with confidence, I left it alone because sometimes as a mom you have to let things ride out.

When he was with the groups he went by another name, but after he became a solo artist he needed a new stage name. As usual, he was in the studio. He was working on his first album. On this particular day while taking a short break, he was speaking to his producers and a few other people that were there and someone asked had he come up with a stage name.

Nahum decided then that if he started with the ABC's he would certainly come up with something.

They were all trying to help, but nothing made sense until my son got to the letter J. Seeing that he had a serious look on his face, his producer asked, "What is it?"

Nahum said nothing but everybody wanted to know what was it about the letter J. That was when he said, "My uncle James was killed a few years ago and I really miss him. He was my favorite uncle so I would like to pay homage to him by using the letter J."

Those in the studio were touched that he loved his uncle that much, others were overwhelmed and they experienced a moment of silence. Afterward they wanted to know, "It [your name] will be J what?"

One of the producers spoke up and said, "You are always in the studio working, but it always seem like a holiday..." And right there, in the wee hours of the morning the name *J. Holiday* was born. The rest is history. My son knew then what he would be called.

I must say it fits. When I first found out what name he'd picked, I asked and my son told me why. I liked it and what it represents. Still, as his mother it took a little while for me to get used to calling him that.

Part of the reason is because J is my brother's initial, and knowing it brought back a flood of memories. So for me it is a profound name, and from here on, I will refer to my son as either *J* or *J. Holiday*.

Raising J. Holiday, A Mother's Untold Story

21 / MAYBE MRS. RIGHT

I was sitting one morning at my home in Sequoyah, when my phone rang. I didn't feel much like having a conversation with anybody so I didn't answer. I was dealing with too many things, including getting ready to move. I thought about how I had never wanted my kids to be sad about anything so I'd kept a keen eye on them, especially my son. I thought about how I had done everything possible to make sure he stayed on the straight and narrow and remained focused on his music.

As the phone rang, I thought about the fact that he'd moved to Atlanta with his group and managers. He had done so because he was determined to make his life and his music work. I knew he was struggling at the time, so I tried my best to always share the little money that I was making. With the phone ringing, I remembered that I'd decided to work a few days a week at my girlfriend's beauty shop. I remembered that on Saturdays I prepared dinners that I could sell to the stylists and the shop clients.

Some Saturdays I would make a hundred dollars. Therefore, if my son would call, I would send him half of what I had. One Saturday I only made fifty dollars. I remembered hoping he wouldn't call that day, because I needed that little piece of change. Still, on that day I'd started thinking about my son, and wound up calling him, just to see what he was up to.

He said things were alright, but I didn't believe him. There was something in his voice that told me he was troubled. So I asked…did he have food? That was when J told me he was eating noodles, with French dressing on them. My heart sank within me. Even though I only had fifty dollars, I sent him twenty five. I had to, and it cost me fifteen dollars more to send it. It didn't matter, because no real mother will let her child go without if she can help. The phone rang again as I remembered that I had been left with ten dollars, but I was ok with that.

The phone kept ringing, so I figured I'd better pick it up. I had no idea it would be my son. At the time, I couldn't tell him what was going on with me, so I simply asked how things were, since he was calling me a little earlier than usual. Feeling like that was strange, I knew something was up.

J wanted to know if a certain young woman that he had gone to school with still lived in the Virginia area. I told him I didn't think so. I had no idea that he'd liked her while they were in high school together, but I said I thought she was married. I also told my son that if she wasn't, and if it was meant to be, I would run into her mom, because I didn't know where the young woman lived.

I remember the year they graduated... The young woman asked my son to sing at the party that her mom was giving for her. Nahum told her he couldn't make it but that his sister would sing for her. It ended up being a nice gradua- tion party, but my son was nowhere to be found. Years later, I found out he wasn't too keen on the fact that the young woman's boyfriend was supposed to have been at the party. I don't blame my son—why would he want to watch the girl he liked, all hugged up with somebody else? Anyway, I had always told my children if they liked some- one and that person was dating someone else; leave that person alone. I know that is good advice. I added, "If it is meant to be, y'all will find each other again."

Well, my son was on his way, with his solo career, but he didn't have a Mrs. Right, so he had called on me. He knew that I would do anything, within legal limits, for him and his sisters. He probably even knew I was very particular about him because I believed he was still fragile from his dad's death. So when he called me that morning, I was sitting there in my chair just kind of half watching TV. I had things to deal with, but none of it included looking for a girl from his past.

I didn't know why he was looking for someone from back in the day, when he could have most any girl he wanted. I think at the time he thought she was special. He might tease me for saying this, but being young, he'd had a crush on her and when he'd been asked to sing at her graduation party, he'd been like "Uh, uh…" He asked his sister if she would take his place, and she did. We didn't find out until years later though that he'd had a thing for that girl. Now he wanted me to find her, and see if she was available. I said I would think about it. I said if it was meant to be, I would eventually run into her mom.

Well after that early phone call, a few weeks passed and I ran into the young woman's mom. I was told that after high school, the young woman had moved to California where she was working and going further in school. Then I figured it was meant to be.

When I talked to my son again, I asked if he'd gotten in touch with the young woman who'd moved to sunny California where tangerines are grown. He said that he and Tangerine had talked on the phone. In time, things happened. Seeing that, I was a happy camper because I didn't want my son to have a lot of baby mamas, or drama. I did not want him to wind up paying out more money than he needed to. Honestly, I really wanted him to wait until he got married, you know, to have sex. Young people think that's old-fashioned, but marriage is honorable and the bed undefiled. That's what the word—the bible—says.

Since my son did otherwise, I just thanked God that he never had heaps of women; he had more sense than that. I hope he continues to keep his head on his shoulders. I hope he remains focused because it wasn't meant for him to have babies in every city where he does a concert. When men decide to take that route, they are only thinking of their greedy selves. I think some males believe it's cute to have babies all over the place, but there's nothing cute or wise about that. You see, I said 'males,' because *a* real *man* wouldn't do those things. A real man is responsible.

He understands that *children need active participating fathers.*

Although there are a lot of women out there, I want my son to use wisdom, in everything he does. That way he will have a lasting career, without a lot of mud attached to him.

The thing that got me about the whole situation with the young woman from high school was that I knew my son had a lot of female friends. It had started when he was little. So when he asked me to find this girl, the one whom we hadn't known had gone to California, I hesitated, at first. Then I finally saw her mom.

I don't know about my son, but *I* had regrets, because things don't always turn out the way we desire them to...

After he became involved with Tangerine, I could see she was frustrated. This was a few years into their relationship. She and I spent a lot of time together, I saw her every day, so I could see that she had no patience. She wasn't wrong in wanting more time from my son, but he didn't have it to give; he was working. When a young man is building his career, he doesn't have a lot of time to devote to a relation-ship. Tangerine knew this, going in. J didn't have the kind of time that other young men who worked a nine to five had. Not only that, he pushed himself to work harder so that those he was responsible for could have more than they would have if he hadn't worked so hard. Whenever something was said, he would always tell me, "I've got to keep working, Ma. I'm on the grind."

Knowing all of this, when Tangerine remained frustrated and needed retail therapy, I spoke to my son about it. However, he kept saying, "Mom she isn't like that," mean-ing she wasn't digging for gold. I took his word for it but I had to tell him, "If you made a wrong call, it is not the end of the world." I just wanted J to be happy. I wanted him to know that in life we make mistakes, but we can still persevere. We can still go on. As a mother, I had also hoped he would get married, but it didn't work out like that, so he and Tangerine went their separate ways. Yet the one good thing that came out of everything was a beautiful girl, one that my son and I love dearly.

When things didn't work out, Tangerine appeared to want to blame my son. When she first opened her mouth and said J messed up her life, I looked that girl square in her face and asked her, "Did he hold a gun to your head?" I asked, "Did he make you leave California?" Then I answered my own question because I knew my son had not been a desperate man. Women were throwing themselves at him! So J hadn't been lacking, he'd just reached back in his past for someone. And just because the situation had grown a little sour, I saw no reason to act ugly; there was a child involved.

I wanted J's happiness. I knew he especially wanted his daughter closer to him. As a man, he would never have chosen to have her living in a house with another man he really didn't know. That was why I told him, "As long as you are doing what you need to do concerning your child, leave the rest to God."

Constantly I prayed for my son, and I will always do so, because there are a lot of she-wolves attempting to get in his path. Many seem like lambs, but God has given us to see that we must steer clear of these people.

To all of the moms out there reading this book, I think the best thing we can do for our kids, especially if it pertains to something like finding an old friend, is stay out of it. I think it is best that our kids find their person themselves. That way, if it doesn't turn out right, we are not to blame.

Now I'm not saying my son blames me for anything, but. what I am saying is disappointment left a bitter taste in my mouth. I didn't want my son to be sad; he had already had a hard time. Then he wound up in a situation where he was called to go to court, although he was doing right. He was never a deadbeat dad. He *never* threw off the responsibility of his child. He made sure that child was taken care of. Being Mr. Nice Guy, he didn't even deny the baby's momma some of the finer material things that *she* wanted too. At the time, I was hoping things could be worked out, but sometimes in the heat of a situation it seems as though people want to get blood out of a turnip.

Still, I'm so glad that my son is a businessman, one who knows how to handle himself. He was prepared. Although I didn't want any of that drama for him, it happened. Now though, he can go on with his life. I know from talking to him after that painful situation that we both see it as a learning experience, for him as well as for me. It is why I wish I had acted on the knowledge that some things are better left alone. I say so because when your child is in pain so are you, unless you are a mom with a heart of stone.

My son is not perfect, in any way. He has flaws, just like the rest of us, but there is one thing I know, even if I don't know anything else... With him actually looking for that particular young woman, he had good intentions. Like any other young man, he's had his share of troubles, but he deals with them, most often in a way that's commendable.

Those of you who are parents know that if you love your kids, you will do whatever it takes to make them happy. You also understand me saying that if I had it to do all over again I probably would not give my son's phone number to Tangerine's mom. I would stay out of it. I would let them get together, or not, on their own. However, I have no animosity in me. How can I, when I have a beautiful, brilliant granddaughter whom I love? And Tangerine and I now have a good relationship. I want only the best for her.

When asked if *he* has any regrets, my son feels the same. His reply is no, he loves his daughter. As a mother, I can't ask for more than that. Still, when I said I wished things had turned out differently, my son said what he always says. At the end of the day, it is what it is.

22 / A WHIRLWIND

I told you that my son's first friend when he got to Atlanta Georgia was a young woman, a Georgia peach that he met at a club. An attractive young lady, Peaches, looked out for my son. They were good friends. Some years later, they became romantically involved, but it didn't work out as well as hoped, because of a few things; you know he was busy getting his career off the ground and she was busy too.

So two years later, from Atlanta my son called me. He spoke about a young woman whom he had known in high school, one he had always admired. During our phone call, I asked why he hadn't dated her. That was when he told me that I had always told him and his siblings "If you like somebody and they are dating someone else, leave them alone. If it's meant to be, it will happen. It will come back around." And you know the story; the young woman had a boyfriend, back when she and my son were in high school...

Well I asked my son what his goals for himself and his potential mate were. I later found out that he wanted them to be like Kimora Lee and Russell Simmons (back when they were a couple). I wasn't surprised because I already knew the type of son I raised, and that was a man of stability, responsibility, love and respect, especially for a woman.

If a man loves his mother, when he finds the right woman, she won't have anything to worry about because he'll love and cherish her too, forever.

So I told you what happened. J and Tangerine didn't work out. Then in Atlanta my son was doing his thing and his friend Peaches was doing hers, so things didn't come together for them either. That's why I was thinking J's life was back on track. I thought that with no woman in the picture he would really be able to concentrate on his career. I mean it had been enough for my son to get over the hurt from his former relationship, but even more pain stemmed from there being a child involved. But the story didn't end there…

My son had been dating Peaches from Atlanta off and on. They were back and forth but she seemed standoffish—to me. I never really got to know her, but at the time, she never really made herself known to me. When someone acts like that, I usually feel they have something to hide. But to be fair, maybe my big voice scared her, or my muscles; you know I work out. Anyway, there was something about Peaches that I couldn't put my hand on. I can't say that she didn't really like my son or maybe even love him, but I do think having a child was the furthest thing from her mind. She had even told me, she wanted no parts of settling down; she wanted to have fun.

When my son became a father, the first time, it was in part because he and Peaches hadn't wanted to settle down. So J had gone in search of the young lady from high school, Tangerine, the one he'd never got a chance to date. Well Peaches found out about my granddaughter when my son went through an ordeal. During that time it took everything within me to keep J calm. I had to remind him over and over to keep a level head. If he wants to give details, you will read them in his book—if he writes one. Anyway, at the time, I could feel the pain he was feeling, because I had felt that type of pain myself, and I wouldn't wish it on my worst enemy.

At that point, due to all the drama, J was vulnerable. He had been through a whirlwind, and I believe Peaches knew this. So after *seven* years, I felt like she decided it was either then or never. My son's guard was down, and I feel that's how he ended up with a second child. I asked, are you freaking kidding me? I couldn't believe it when I was told. I was hurt, for him, but what could I do?

I had a talk with Peaches and asked her what was she trying to do? When she replied, I wasn't satisfied with her answer.

My son always tells me that she wasn't out for what she could get from him. Yet as a mother, I must tell you the truth; I always have my doubts—about everyone, until they prove me wrong. I especially had them when Peaches told my son, after she became pregnant, that she wasn't taking a baby back to her small apartment, but then I realized. That was her prerogative. It was her and my son's business.

Now when my son finally told me Peaches was pregnant *and* that she was moving in with him, my heart sank, all the way down to the floor. I was devastated because by this time I believed he was in fear mode. By that I mean since he had just been through an ordeal he did not want to ever go through anything like that again. So I thought he felt like this time his child would be in the house with him. So I reminded him of what I'd always told him... I had often said he should not give women keys to his home. I said, "Once they get in, and if things aren't working fine, you'll have to deal with getting them out."

After J and I talked I realized there was nothing I could do other than pray. Now this is where the interesting part comes in. He told me that he wanted me and Peaches to have a good relationship. I welcomed that. I even told him I didn't mind, but that Peaches would have to communicate more. I couldn't even get that young woman to answer a text from me, and forget her calling me, back then.

Anything that my son asked me to do—within the legal limits—I was willing to do, because I knew he needed my help. So I reached out. I told Peaches that she could talk to me about anything, and I meant it.

Then all of a sudden, since Peaches was with my famous son, her mama comes up and thinks she's going to shut *me* out of the picture; at least that's how I felt.

In the beginning I felt as though the mama and one of her siblings tried to form a block-out. I felt like they were attempting to make sure I couldn't keep my own grand-baby. This mess went on for a good portion of my grand-baby's first year. I was hurt—and hot! I was steaming with anger. I felt like a ditch had been dug, but I also feel like this. If someone is digging a ditch for me to fall in, they just might fall in, face-first; if I hold my peace.

I wondered who they were used to dealing with. I felt they had it twisted if they thought I was that person because the last time I checked *J. Holiday* was, and is, *my* son. I am also confident in one thing; he always will be. Can't nothing or no one come between us. I know that's grammatically incorrect, but you get the picture.

I told the mama and others that they were in my son's house, only because he had allowed Peaches to move in with him. I said, "If any of you have thoughts of control-ling anything here, think again, because the only thing you can control is your place back where you came from."

As I sat thinking on all these things, some of which were hurtful to me, I remembered what I had always told my children... *Keep your dignity; never stoop to anyone else's level.* Then I had to remember to take my own advice.

Since I've done that, Peaches and I have been getting along fine. She is a good mother. We've grown closer; we communicate, and have a nice relationship. My youngest granddaughter is something else too! She's walking and talking and I get to see her often. I love her so much, just like I love all my grandchildren.

23 / THE LABEL

When my son got signed to Capitol Records he was happy and so was I. Still, I feel they never backed him like a label should have. He did three video shoots for three different songs and everything was going okay until they realize that my son wasn't like the talent-less artist. He wasn't going to do just anything for a dollar. If I didn't know any better, I would say that people at his own record label were jealous of him.

They didn't push his first album like they should have, and they didn't push the second one at all. By that I mean they didn't promote him and get the word out about the album the way they often do other artists. My son actually told me that he was going to have to push and promote his second album. When he said that I knew he wouldn't be with that label for much longer.

I wasn't sure how true it was that the label wasn't doing all that they could, until I was out at the stores shopping. I was also checking to see if his album was in the 'new re-lease' section. If his CD was there and if it had the bar code and price tag covering his face, I peeled it off and replaced it where buyers could see my son's face. I did it right in front of the store managers who would ask, "Who are you?" I would say, "I'm from the label."

Once when his first album was released I didn't see it on shelves so I asked a worker to go in back and see if it was there. They did and came out and put them on display. I wasn't about to leave until they did. Then I bought the first copy. But back to what I was saying…in this particular chain store, I mentioned that *J. Holiday* had a third album coming out. Some of the shoppers and others working in the store overheard and looked at me like I had said something wrong. Seeing that those people had been unaware, I was pissed off at those who work at the record label. I felt like I could have flown to New York to get a few things straight. I thought about it though, and decided I wasn't about to lower my standards.

I asked my son a few months before he left that label, what his plans were. He spoke plainly. Either they were going to give him what he wanted or he was leaving. Well he did just that, and I applaud him because he understands that you can't let people mistreat you or back you into a corner. Allowing either of those things is never good.

The label wanted to change him into a clean cut guy, wearing a suit, no braids and no beard. But no one will make my son do anything until he is ready. The label didn't like that, so I feel that is why they made things rough for him. He wouldn't bow to them, but he did bow *out* of the label.

At the time of this writing, *J. Holiday* was working on his third album. I believe he will go straight to the top whether he's signed to a label or not. In other words, no matter how things seem, you can never give up, it doesn't matter what positive thing you are trying to do.

Sure, my son runs into things from time to time that cause a little standstill, but that happens to all of us. It seems to be the way in life. The main thing is to not let any given situation get the best of you.

One thing I know for sure is you've got to keep pressing toward your goals. You can never give up, no matter the task. If someone tells you that you can't, look them in the eyes and say with authority, 'I know I can.' All of us have a purpose in this life. We just need to discover what it is and walk it out.

24 / A LESSON LEARNED

When my son was growing up, he loved Michael Jackson's music. He could sing a lot of the songs and do a lot of the dances, including the moonwalk. He was about six or seven and he was carrying on! He loved The King of Pop. Even with him loving Michael Jackson it still never dawned on me that my boy was a rising star in the making. However, since he was so crazy about the entertainer, I decided to purchase the *Moonwalker* VHS tape for my son's eighth birthday, and boy was he happy!

While he was growing up he kept it near him and watched it every day. I have to tell you that I loved it too, but as a parent, I got tired of it. Parents you know how that is; yet I watched it with him. When my son became a teenager he began to like all types of music and a multitude of artists including Marvin Gaye and Donny Hathaway.

When Michael Jackson passed away, I was talking to my son about the entertainer's death, and also about a dream I'd had a few years back. In the dream, Michael Jackson and I were discussing his *Thriller* album, and about the fact that so many people were hating on him. In my dream I told Michael not to worry. I also stated, "As long as people are talking about you, you are doing well." I said that to mean he was still on their minds.

In real life, outside of the dream I continued speaking to my son. I said, "Look how big Michael became." I also sadly told him, "Since MJ is dead I will never get to see him in person." I further explained that I felt my dream had been a message from God. This I shared with my son, adding that he too would be famous, like MJ.

After our conversation my son asked me if he could have the *Moonwalker* videotape back. He said, "Ma, I really need it."

I agreed but I told him I needed a copy.

I will tell you something. It has been a few years since The King of Pop left us, and I ain't seen my videotape yet!

During the early years of my son's career, there wasn't a lot of extra money rolling in, so we had to figure out ways to get to his different shows. Thinking about it reminds me of an incident I will never forget, because I can still remember the smell in that dirty car. It was a stale smell I'm sure, from previous renters.

It was a bright and sunny Saturday in July. I wanted to attend my son's outdoor concert at Druid Hill Park in Maryland. The thing was I had no way to get there. My only choice was to rent a car from a man at a local budget place where I should have known never to rent a bike from, much less a car.

Anyway, time was winding down and I needed a way to get to my son's performance. My daughter, my grandson, and my granddaughter were with me and we were all excited about going to the concert. In the past I'd rented cars from the place and the man that I mentioned, but each vehicle had always had something wrong with it, in one way or another. But I rented from that man again because I could pay cash and he was within walking distance.

The car I rented that morning was the straw that broke the camel's back. Not only was it dirty and the trunk wouldn't open, but there was strong sharp musky odor assaulting me and my family's nostrils. It was a terrible experience, up there with some of the worst I've encountered. I tried to spray that car—with perfume from my purse, to get the odor out, but to no avail. I just made it worse.

Finally I found the problem…a used prophylactic between the seats! I was discreet when I tossed it, and my family and I finished the trip. I told no one about that incident, not until now. Yet I hope when people read this chapter, the rental car man's business is bankrupt—if he still doesn't care enough about his customers to make sure they receive clean and secure cars from him.

When I returned that car I told the rental place owner that he should take care and clean his cars. I really wanted to say that I should whip him up and down the street for renting that unclean vehicle to me. But I did something with more impact. I haven't rented from him since.

Looking back, I simply thank God that my family and I were able to get to the park where my son was performing.

Now days, things are very different for me. I can rent any type of car I desire. Yet now I'm careful when I make decisions, about everything. I pray. Now, no matter how badly I would like to do something, before I'll rent from a less than reputable company, count me out. I'd rather start walking, and prayerfully a Good Samaritan will come along to help me.

Raising J. Holiday, A Mother's Untold Story

25 / LIGHTS, CAMERAS, ACTION!

October 25th, 2006 was a day I will always remember. That was the day my son had his first video shoot—exciting! Not only was he shooting his first video, for his single *Be With Me*, but it was being shot at a historic greasy spoon in Washington D.C.

The practice run started about 5am that morning. The team was combing through the final details before they would start shooting the video. I arrived later that morning bright and early with my daughters and grandkids. We were all excited to be a part of that great day. We had never seen so many big trucks, cameras, old cars, and other things.

As soon as I spotted my son's manager I wanted to know which of the trailers were his. He told me and I went because I wanted J to know I was there. I tell you I have never been more proud of him than I was that day. My son had taken over the subway; the U street corridor between 12th and 13th Streets was shut down.

There isn't too much that excites my son, but that day it was different, I could see stars in his eyes. He was happy that this was finally happening for him, after so much hard work and long hours. The streets were lined with people from all walks of life, leaving hardly any room to move. Everybody wanted to know what all the fuss was about and why all the cameras, old cars, and big trucks were there. Before I could answer anyone, an elderly lady walked over to me and said, "I don't know who ***J. Holiday*** is, but he must be important, because it is hard for anyone to get us to shut down the eatery. The last time we shut down was when Denzel Washington shot the movie, The Pelican Brief," eight years prior.

I was very proud when she made that statement about my son, although she had no idea that I was the mama. That older woman looked at me and said, "You know this young man?" I felt puffed up with pride, but very humbly I said, "He is my son." She said, "I will tell you one thing, he is well-mannered and his career will go far." She was very surprised that I was so calm with all of that happening for my son. I thanked her and said I would come by and have lunch with her sometime, and I did. What she didn't know was that I was just as honored talking to her. When she said the greasy spoon hadn't shut down in eight years, I knew then that my son would go to the top, just like Denzel.

When I think about that very cold day in October, I still get full of joy. It didn't matter how often I looked at my son that day, he had such a gleam in his eyes. However, one thing I kept thinking was about his dad. I was sad that he wasn't there to see his son take flight. But still the world would get the opportunity to see what I already knew, that my son would become what he was born to be.

As soon as the cameras got a glimpse of my son they began rolling. The video shoot took a total of about twenty hours to complete, but the girls and I didn't care. We would have stayed to the bitter end to make sure he was ok. Plus it was exciting to be a part of it all, because it was my son. I even got a ticket that night. When I left it was on my car. I felt a little upset, but the feeling vanished. The day had been perfect. I wasn't going to have it ruined.

Since I have always been a pretty laid back person, no one was aware who *J. Holiday's* mom was. Therefore, I had to step up, out of the crowd and make myself known. It was my son's day and I wanted the attention to be on him, but he wanted the world to know that his mom and sisters were present for the roll call.

My son was shooting his first video entitled *Be With Me*, and he had a beautiful video vixen to share the day with him. Everybody kept asking me who was *J. Holiday* and where did he come from? I would tell them.

Then some people were asking why he didn't have a dark-skinned vixen in the video with him. My reply was, "What difference does it make, as long as the girl is suitable for the video?" Some people are always trying to start something.

The food and drinks were free that day, so anyone could walk around and eat anything they wanted; even some homeless people came through. Most were having a good time, until this man started to push his way through the crowd. But he had to get it together, or leave, because nobody was going to rain on my son's parade, not that day. Then there were some workers who were helping with the shoot. They started trying to order each other around. I figured some people will act up no matter where they are.

Since that was the first time in my life being at a video shoot, I had no idea they would shoot scenes over and over. I asked my son was he tired of shooting the same scene. His reply was, "They do that so they can pick the best ones for the final draft." That was my son's day and he deserved to get the attention, but there will always be people trying to get their fifteen seconds of fame. I wasn't going to put up with that, so I pulled my son's manager to the side and spoke to him about it. I told him, "Either you tell them to get it together, or I will," because those people were not going to do that on my watch.

My son had to smooth my ruffled feathers, because I was getting a little bothered. He even jokingly said, "Ma, you gonna have to go, if you don't calm down."

A woman we knew, and her daughter, were trying to be seen too. They had always said they were like family. Well this woman even went so far as to claim she was *J. Holiday*'s mom, but she did it when I stepped away. Then a feminine man spoke up. He said, "No. That is not his mom." He said, "I saw *her* earlier." That man also cynically asked, about the woman who'd lied, "And who did her weave?" When I returned, my girls told me they were embarrassed for the woman and her daughter.

The shoot had been going on for about ten hours, and people were yet arriving. I know some were coming to be noisy. Others arrived with their entire families because they'd heard there was free food. There were drinks too and a good time. I heard someone else make another comment about *J. Holiday* needing to have a darker girl in the video. I was itching to say something because it was obvious that the video vixen was African-American, but I held my peace, because it was my son's day and I didn't want to spoil it. The day was finally coming to a close, and I was happy because I had gotten a little tired, but it was a day that I will always have in my memory. That was the day when the world actually got a glimpse of *J. Holiday* and what he was capable of.

It was about a month before I saw the video for the first time on 106 and Park, a music show on BET, Black Entertainment Television. The station presents videos of new artists; they called them 'the new joint of the day.' When I saw the video for the first time I was probably more excited than my son! *Be With Me* didn't get the buzz that my son was expecting and he was a disappointed. I told him, "Not to worry, you will get a song that will shock the world and make them stand at attention." I was right. Within a month's time there was a buzz that a new single was on the horizon. When I heard the song for the first, without seeing the video, I told him straight up that song will be a hit, and it was. He shot the video in the desert in LA.

This time when it was shown on BET, it stayed there for a total of forty-six days, and it was at number one. After that the haters came out of the woodwork! But it was no big deal, nor was it news to him. I told Nahum, "When people are not talking about you, check yourself," I told my son, "Forget them haters. No matter how much people talk, don't get into beefs with anyone, and whatever you do— don't stoop to no one's lower level."

I recently heard him in an interview where he said he would do nothing to embarrass his mother. That's awesome.

Then somebody put out a rumor saying that my son's song was meant for another artist. I won't call his name, but it was said that the other artist's people wanted to buy the song back. Please. I told my son, "That song was for you, because you are the one singing it." I had to pray though because people will create something stupid out of nothing. Finally that blew over and things ended well. I always told my son, "Never worry about what others are doing, because you will get what God has for you."

Right after the song *Bed* went to the top, about a month later, my son came out with another single title entitled 'Suffocate,' which had a video shot in Paris. *Ooh la la*. I didn't get a chance to attend, but it was a success. This song ended up on the BET count down too. My son is doing very well, and as long as he doesn't let what people say get in his head, I know he will continue on to the top. I have always told him and his sisters that people talked, and are yet talking about Jesus, but He became the king of kings. I also told my son, "You weren't born a copycat, so always have your own identity."

With reference to the *Be With Me* video shoot, I was so happy that two of my nephews arrived to be a part of my son's special day. Those two were walking around, acting like they were already big shot security for their cousin. They were making sure that in between the shoots that my son was well taken care of.

During the breaks, there was the inviting smell of hot dogs, beans, and burgers floating in the air. It was just a day where no one seemed to notice the cold weather. We were just there to experience history. We didn't care about double parked cars, bikes, or baby strollers. We just wanted more action out of the video shoot. I wanted everyone to know about it, from D.C. to Spain, because that was a long awaited day for my son.

It didn't matter to me whether it was raining, sleeting or snowing, if my son had something going on, I was going to be there, unless he told me not to come to that event. From time to time, he feels that the crowd at a particular venue might be a little off the chain. He sometimes feels that I don't need to be there. He is protective of me that way. When he first told me not to show up, I'll tell you…I was not too happy. I understood, but I realized it was enough for security to watch him, so it would be too much for them to have to deal with me too. I didn't need my son jumping off the stage because of me.

At an altogether different venue in Maryland, J was to perform near the water front. Even after security told the men at the door who I was, they still gave me a problem. I told my son's bodyguard that I could handle it, and not to bother my son. I said I could give that dude at the door a left hook. By the time I heard about it again, my son had told his bodyguard that he'd better straighten things out because that's why he was being paid.

It didn't matter where I went to see my son perform, people would see the bouncer at the door speaking with me, and allowing the people with me to enter. Then I would wind up with a group of unknowns trying to get in with me. They would lie, and claim they were **J. Holiday's** brother, sister, aunt—whoever. After a while, it became funny, and I wouldn't pay those people any mind. They will always be there.

26 / BACK OF MY LAC/ROUND II

Have you ever in your life been in such a state of mind that you didn't know whether to cry, run, or just ride around town to get your thoughts together? Well this is what happened to my son, the man who is now known around the globe as *J. Holiday*.

Often I was concerned about him becoming depressed, since I'd never gotten a clear picture of how he was dealing with his dad's death. That had taken a toll on all of us, especially my son. I didn't really find out how much it affected him until after the first album dropped and I heard the first song. When I heard his first line, I said, "*What*?!" I pressed pause and took a minute to gather my thoughts, because I couldn't believe what I'd just heard. Then I started the song over. I realized my son had his own feelings that I hadn't known about, simply because he hadn't talked to me about them. He'd always said, "Ma, I don't want to worry you." As a good son, he had often said too, "Ma, I'm alright." He even says it now. Still, back then I knew he wasn't.

That album was great, but on his first track anyone could tell that he didn't feel the situation with his father had been to his liking because of what he said about his dad.

Some people who knew him felt he disrespected his dad. They argued that, "Butch was a good man—J shouldn't be talking about his dad like that." I had to set people straight because only my son's sisters and I knew what really happened. People somehow got the notion that Butch left me—that he just walked out on us, his family. However, in an interview my son clarified things. He let it be known that his father had a *heart attack*. My son also candidly delved further into an issue that is intensely personal. He let it be known that he felt that his father could have told us, the family, that he was sick. In the same interview my son revealed that he was angry because his father hadn't told anybody—not even me, his mother.

My son also said that while his father lived, all his father had to do was have an operation to fix the problem. J has let it be known that if he had one wish, it would be to bring his father back. That I understand…because I have felt the same way, countless times, especially within the last eight years. My son is now a father. What son would not want his own father to be part of his children's lives? My son would love to ask his father certain questions. Every son needs the guidance of his father, although all are not blessed to have this. Some sons have mentors, but it's not the same thing as having your own good father.

The devastation of losing his dad at the age of eleven was unbearable at times. I knew this without my son saying anything to me. All I had to do was look at him and his pain was visible. It was all over his face. As a young black man, he would have highly benefitted from his father's wisdom and love, even though Butch had already taught J many things and gave him lasting memories.

My son probably saw my pain too. That was the only period in my life when I didn't know what to say to my son. He was so quiet. I didn't know how to help him, because I needed help too.

At this particular time he was still living at home. Then he ventured out and got his own apartment. He was also with his singing group. Then later, in the summer of 2003 the group left for Atlanta, where they would pursue their music career. I told you before that things never took off with the group, so my son went solo.

Immediately, he started writing lyrics for his own album, but things were hectic. Things were hard, but he made the best of everything. He even put a lot of the pain that he had known into his first album. It was called

Back Of My Lac. I know he had to put his energy somewhere, and using it that way turned out to be a great idea.

I even saw on RapMusic.com where they spoke of that
album saying *J. Holiday* had joined prestigious company.
Mentioned were Janet Jackson and her brother Michael
Jackson's *You Rock My World,* before the author of the
article spoke of my son's song *Bed.* It entered the Urban
AC chart at number 24. At the time that was the highest
debut by a new act since the year 1995.

Yet many days before the project was finished my son
would sit in the back of his lac (his Cadillac) writing songs
for his album. Some days I would call to see what he was
doing. Some days he didn't feel like writing anything so
he would cruise down the boulevard, just thinking about
his life and where he was headed. On the days that he really felt like writing, he would write a complete song, but if
he wasn't exactly pleased with it he would continue to
revise it until he felt the form was perfect.

That was a hard album to write because he was dealing
with the pain of his father's death and wondering whether
or not he would be successful as a solo artist. Although
my son and I would talk just about every day, but I hadn't
known how devastated my son was until just before his
album dropped. We had a mother-to-son talk and he spoke
of how hard it was, and how much it took for him to complete that first album.

He said to me, "Whether it's successful or if it's a flop, I
know you'll be there."

I felt very proud that my son knew I would be there for
him no matter what, win or lose. Many people say 'mother
knows best,' but in in a lot of cases that doesn't ring true.
Still, a mother that is close to their children will know
when they are in in trouble...

Just before the album's release he was so frustrated that it
took all I had within me to keep my son calm. I told him
that when things are held up, there is a reason.

I wanted him to hold his peace, and I always had to pull out a scripture. I knew he would listen to me. I also knew that I could cause calm to wash over him.

There were times that he wanted to give up, but I wouldn't allow it. I told him, "You have to hang in there." I said "Trust me, when your album drops, it will take the world by storm."

I was right, because when my son's album was released, the world asked, who is *J. Holiday* and where did he come from? One hip hop news writer called my son intriguing and said he was equal parts soldier and sage. That writer said the preacher's son—meaning J—had chosen R&B as his pulpit.

Then the bootleggers came out, but despite them his album did great. Don't get his momma twisted because I turned in as many of them as possible. Had people not known who I was before the album dropped, the bootleggers did, and they will tell you, "That lady ain't to be played with, but she is someone to be reckoned with."

Speaking of his albums, my son's first CD did quiet well—even after the label didn't do all they could have to aid it to go straight to the top. His second is called *Round II* and he and I had many conversations about it. I was aware that the label had not planned to promote that album, because they wanted to change him completely, but let me tell you something. As J's mom I know that my son will never be anybody's puppet, I don't care who they are. If you're not God, get to stepping.

The label soon found out the same thing, the hard way, just like everybody else. He told me on several occasions I don't care how much money you want to pay me if I'm not comfortable with it I'm not doing it. My son does things in his own time. *Round II* did the same thing that *Back of my Lac* did, and that was being the most added single at Urban Mainstream radio. His first single on that album was *It's Yours*. Now *J. Holiday* is still on the grind, working on another project.

27 / A THIRTY YEAR SECRET

Thirty years have passed and in my life many things have happened. I never got over my husband's sudden death. I even married a man that reminded me of him. I was able to let Butch's passing lie dormant for about eight years, but when my second marriage ended, all of the old wounds came whooshing back like a rushing wind. I felt the pain that had never really left, and I felt like I began to die deep within my soul.

I still had no idea what had really caused Butch's sudden departure. I know that when people die like he did, there has to be a cause. No matter where I was or what I was doing there were always questions in the back of my mind. One day I was on my way out of town and I got a text from my son. We always texted each other everyday, but this was a little different. The most intriguing thing was what the text said. He wanted me to check into some incident that took place in Vietnam while his dad fought in the war.

Me being the private investigator that I am, I began to dig deep into the information I had just been given by my son. As I searched, I found that by the end of the day I was devastated all over again. However, I was determined to find out the cause of my husband's demise and what had brought it on for him and thousands and thousands of other men and women who'd fought in the Vietnam War.

I quickly gave news of the information I received to my son and his sisters. I felt they had the right to know what had caused their father to be taken from them so suddenly. While he fought in the war he'd contracted heart disease. It was caused by a chemical called Agent Orange. Since that is its code name, it is better known as Operation Ranch Hand and was used by the U.S. military.

It was given its name from the color of the orange-striped barrels that it was shipped in. As part of an herbicidal warfare agenda, it was sprayed from helicopters or from low-flying C-123 Provider aircrafts fitted with pump systems and chemical tanks. The goal was to strip the forestry that provided cover for guerilla fighters. The spraying was also supposed to destroy the ability of the peasants to support themselves in the countryside. Then maybe they would flee to the U.S. If they did, then the guerillas wouldn't have support from those people and the guerillas wouldn't have a food supply.

Many of those things happened *and* this herbicidal warfare destroyed countless U.S. Vietnam veterans, servicemen and women who served their country. Some studies show that veterans who served in the South during that war have increased rates of cancer and respiratory disorders. Military people who loaded airplanes and helicopters used in Ranch Hand were more heavily exposed. People like Butch, a trained Sentry Dog Handler and Airman, are believed to have had some of the heaviest exposure.

Not until my research did I discover that fighting in the Vietnam War was the cause of my husband's heart problem, because I really hadn't known he had one. Then I found out many years after he was gone. I feel so bad sometimes because he was only twenty two years old when he was in the service. Being that young, he could not have dreamed what he would face.

So now I know that my husband was slowly deteriorating, even when we first got married. It took me thirty years to realize why my Butch was so sick all those years. To me it seemed so unfair because he wasn't even drafted for the war; he went in someone else's place. He also told me when I first met him that he wanted to get out of Maryland, because it was boring. He wasn't the only one who wanted a change because I didn't care for Lexington Park either, and neither did my children. When we went on holidays to visit Butch's parents I always looked forward to his mom's Thanksgiving and Christmas dinners, and her thirty day cakes. They really took thirty days to make. The cakes were delicious, but my mother-in-law had to set the juice aside. Then she set the fruit aside, and other ingredients. I didn't know what all she did, but the cake that was like a fruit cake took thirty days to make. Still, my kids didn't like to go to their grandmother's home, because she only let them play one tabletop game. And since she only had that one game, my kids dubbed it 'The Game.'

Due to all the new information, I can now better appreciate the way my husband was towards me when it came to certain things. I wanted him to take us skating, bike riding, jogging—just anything that involved the family, but he wouldn't do any of that. He always had an excuse. I didn't know why at the time, but I later found out it would have been too much for his heart. In his way, he had been attempting to protect us. I knew he desired to do those things with us, but now I know his heart wouldn't let him. For him to be taken away from us away so soon was bad enough, but finding out the reason made matters worse for me.

My husband would talk about Vietnam and how he was taught to kill children as well as adults. Soldiers like him were taught to shoot anything that moved. I felt so bad for him. At home, Butch would have nightmares, all the time. He would be fighting in his sleep and I would have to shake him out of them. When he woke he would be sweaty and he told me he was running from the enemy. I would remind him that he was not in Vietnam anymore.

With this newfound information about the ischemic heart disease that Butch had contracted in while in the war, I realized 'the enemy' wound up living within him for the next fourteen years, until it got the best of his heart. He might have known for a while, but I surely didn't, and I will never forget how shocked I was when he died because he'd said he would live until he was one hundred and twenty-five. Looking back, I now realize he knew his days were numbered. All those years he'd had me fooled.

Raising J. Holiday, A Mother's Untold Story

28 / THE PREDICAMENT

In a prior chapter I stated how my son wanted me to find a certain young woman for him—the one from his past. I told you how I did. The truth of the matter was that he had another friend. Remember Peaches, in Atlanta? Well she became his girlfriend. Yet they kept breaking up, going back and forth, dancing 'round and 'round.

During one of their break-ups, I found out after speaking with Peaches that she just wanted to have fun. She wanted to be with her friends. At the time, she wasn't ready to settle down. This I was told after my son's baby -momma drama. So what could Peaches say about it? After all, she'd had no intention of settling down, and my son couldn't make up his mind. So during his and Peaches' break-up he'd gotten involved with the young woman who could have been Mrs. Right.

After all that happened, it turned out that Peaches decided that she wanted a child by my son. Well she could have done that in the beginning. But that's the way the cookie crumbled.

I think if we all had to do it all over again, we might think twice. Then again maybe not, because things worked out for the best.

Well anyway, you know how mothers always know things before they even get the truth out of their children? Well, in January my son mentioned that he had something to talk to me about. I said I was ready whenever he had the time. You see, I already knew something was up because he'd brought Peaches to my house for the first time. Therefore, I knew she was either pregnant, or J was going to tell me he was engaged—but that didn't set right with me, so I figured it was the first thing.

Days went by, and finally J told me, but not by phone or even through e-mail; my son had the nerve to inform me of something as important as a baby on the way in a text! I'm telling you, I read it over and over again, hoping I was dreaming or that I'd misread the text. I read it again, and it began to sink in. Not only was Peaches from Atlanta pregnant, like I had already known, but my son said they were moving in together. He and I texted back and forth, and as his mother, I reminded him of what I had always told him... I'd said he should not give women keys to his home. I said, "If it doesn't work out, you may have a problem getting her out of your house."

I had nothing against the new young woman, Peaches, but I knew my son needed to make sure this was what he wanted, before he made such a drastic move. I asked had he thought it through, baby or not. We texted back and forth that night, and he said one thing to me that I have not forgotten. It was, "Mom I'm still scared of you."

I said "You don't have to be afraid of me; I'm not God, nor do I have a heaven or hell to put you in."

Really, I don't think my son is afraid of me, not in any scary sense, but I think he just has a certain level of respect for me. For that I am grateful. One thing I know, even if I don't know anything else is that my son loves me and nobody or nothing will come between us. We have a good relationship. Sure, women have entered his life, but the last time I checked, I was the one who birthed him, and I'm the only person, other God, who knows him best.

My son has told the world that I gave him a good foundation. If you've done the same for your child or children, then all that we as parents can do is allow our kids to grow and find their way. Trust me, when they need us they will call or come by and that's ok.

Looking back, I have one thought. I am very proud of the man that my son has become, and I know that as long as he stays humble and puts God first, he will go a long way in life. There is nothing that he will not be able to accomplish. Of course I want the same for my daughters. One is in the studio working on new music, while the other has achieved her bachelor's degree.

Whatever my kids decide to do in life, I just want them to be happy.

Raising J. Holiday, A Mother's Untold Story

29 / LIFE LESSONS

As a parent, I have often wished things in my life had turned out differently, but I also feel that children don't need to be stuck smack in the middle of drama. That is why I am offering the following life lessons. Some are questions you can ask yourself. Others are statements that will hopefully make you think and help you make good choices for you and your child.

1. My advice… Men, when you see a beautiful face, or women, when you see a handsome face, first get to know that person, before you do anything as serious as go to bed with them. And don't—by any means—be quick to have a baby. Too many people get sexually involved without really knowing each other. They think 'wham, bam, thank you ma'am.' Then after that the drama usually starts.

2. Parents, when kids come into your lives remember; it is no longer just about you. The main thing now should be your child.

3. There is something we must all realize. In situations involving children and support, the person who wants exorbitant sums of money is often the mother, not the child, because a child will only receive whatever their mother gives them.

4. Parents, if you're arguing, *think* if there is a child or children involved. Think of them, and not just only about yourself and what you want. Remember that children get caught in the middle.

5. Mothers and fathers, if you want to drag your child's other parent into court, stop and think. Also ask yourself *'how will this affect my child?'*

6. Parents, ask yourselves '*am I so determined to make things bad for the other person that I will actually wind up digging a deeper hole for myself?*'

7. Women, don't be so desperate and needy. Don't have men in and out of you and your children's lives. That only confuses your kids and keeps negative stuff going.

8. Remember, when people do things for spite it normally backfires right in their face.

9. Parents, learn to tell your kids no. Say it and stick to it. I love my kids but I had to make sure I said no when I needed to.

10. When negative situations come, remind your self, *this too will pass.*

11. I was just discussing with my daughter how proud I am of her. At the time of this writing, she had a fifteen year old son. After she had him, she made up her mind that she wasn't going to have any more kids until she gets married. Plus she decided she wasn't pressed to have different men hanging around her son. I find that to be wonderful because the truth of the matter is that women who do otherwise are not doing it for the interest of their child.

12. Women often keep company with any ol' body either to please their own flesh or just to say they have a man. Not Good. Don't be desperate, needy or greedy.

13. If you are getting child support, consider your child or children before you try and make things bad for the other parent.

14. As I've said before, when a child becomes part of the equation, then their parent or parents need to take a back seat and stop being so press and selfish.

15. All I can say to any young lady out there is that *it takes two to tango*, and unless the person raped you, when you have a child, you are just as responsible for that child as the man.

16. When you make a decision to try and get back at someone consider your child first.

17. Patience is a virtue, one that we all need.

18. Learn to pray. When it comes to your children and grandchildren, if something is not right , ask God to move it or give them strength while He lets them go through it.

19. I have often told my son to keep his cool because God is in control. Since God is in control, and since He will fight your battles, do what I have told my son. *Stand behind the battle line*. Watch God work things out.

20. I have always told my kids, Before you do anything, always try and think of the advantages *and* the disadvantages. If the disadvantages outweigh the advantages, then *run*—as fast as you can in the opposite direction!

21. I have always told all three of my children, Never stoop to anyone else's level. Let things play out. Be patient and let things be.

THINGS I LEARNED FROM MA

By my eldest daughter

We affectionately call our mother 'Ma.' She may have a tough exterior, but I know that she has a heart of gold. Over the years I have witnessed her give those in need her last and sometimes go without herself.

She also has a gift for working with the mentally handicapped and physically disabled. I didn't appreciate everything that she did for me while growing up, because for some reason, I always wished I was born with a silver spoon in my mouth. However, now that I am married with three children of my own, I appreciate and marvel at everything she did for me. Even though we sometimes faced adversity, she always kept our little family together and for that I am grateful.

My mother is also a pretty and stylish woman; when I was a teenager many of the guys thought she was my sister. I didn't like that then, but now that I have a teenage daughter of my own I appreciate it because I too have retained my youthful appearance.

My mother is also a Licensed Cosmetologist who often states that she has 'growing hands.' I have witnessed this too; although she experimented on my kinky hair when I was younger, I have had times when my hair would begin to 'grow down my back' as they say.

Ma would often quickly tell someone that they were 'not all that' or that their food was 'nothing to write home about.' She is very witty and can make the simplest story entertaining. I also find it amazing how she remembers stories and poetry from her youth, verbatim, especially a dance where she still remembers every step. It's called *Working in A Coal Mine.*

Ma is a character and very creative. Don't get her started talking about how she danced on a television show called *Harambe* with a group call The Black Heritage Dancers. Just play the right song in the right environment and she will give you a modern dance performance that you thought came straight from Alvin Ailey.

My mother also has what some would call a 'third eye.' She calls it a discerning spirit. She's also a dreamer, so she would have dreams about things that would happen in the future. This explains why she always seems to know what I was about to do before I did it. That really bothered me growing up; I stayed on punishment.

My mother's main motto is *to trust God and let him guide you*; she has strong faith and notes that *prayer changes things*. I have witnessed this at many times in my adult life. Although my mother is entertaining and has strong religious beliefs; one of the best things that I learned from her is how to persevere.

That used to be one her favorite saying, "You have to per-severe." I know now that means never give up. Ma always made me believe that anything was possible and that I could accomplish anything that I put my mind to. That alone has inspired me to continue to pursue my dreams in spite of the obstacles.

As she would say "What God has for you, no man can take away."

Quineice Clarkson

MY MOTHER

by my baby daughter

I can describe the beautiful woman I call mom. She is count-less things, including a woman of many words and phrases, power, strength, compassion, and encouragement. Growing up, I was pretty quiet, reserved, and fearful of *everything*. Thanks to my mom bringing me up in a strong household, I can accomplish *anything*. My mom has kept me from falling when I was (*mentally*) bending over and intentionally aiming for the ground. She is every-thing to me and *I* am a wonderful person and mother be-cause of her.

A Woman of Many Words
The main thing I remember about my mom is how she talked to us growing up. This was not your regular conver-sation that other families might engage in. My mom had a way with words and used idioms and interesting phrases when she spoke to us. For example, when mom talked to us about life and issues we were facing, she responded to us differently from other parents. She used phrases like *"If the shoe fits, wear it," "That was the straw that broke the camel's back," "Kill two birds with one stone,"* and *"I'm going to be on you like white on rice."* The 'white on rice' phrase affected me intensely. I knew that could *not* have been a good thing so I did not want to test her. With a strong voice, and a profound, direct statement like that, who would 'try' my mother? Now, I laugh every day when

I think of these and many other idioms or phrases she used as her own special way of talking to her children.

Power and Strength
My mother is a woman of great power and strength. I am not saying this because she is my mom, but because I have seen it with my own eyes. It is amazing how her immediate family seeks her for advice and her decision-making abilities regarding family issues. I remember the phone ringing and on the line was one of her many siblings, asking how she would handle a situation. They took heed. The power is in her walk and definitely her talk. She speaks with authority and walks in any place with confidence. Over the years, I have gained the *strength and power* my mom has because I really had no choice. I mean, she is my mom; a woman who will be around me forever until we leave this earth. Besides, *"The apple does not fall too far from the tree,"* right? My mom has a power that connects her to, and influences every individual she encounters.

Compassion and Encouragement
My mother is a woman of compassion and encouragement. I grew up in a religious family. Even though while growing up, my siblings and I did not fully understand the bible, religious philosophies, and my mother's faith, there was a message behind it all. She always told me "God will provide anything you ask for." She encouraged me to read the bible so that I would understand biblical scriptures and stories for myself. My mom wanted to make sure her children had a spiritual upbringing no matter how we would end up later. I had my bouts of rebellion and tribulations, but today, I can look back at what my mom instilled in me. She has been there for me all of my life, guiding me through single motherhood, school, relationships, and so much more. I have no idea where I would be today if my mom did not encourage me to stay off the streets, away from drugs, prostitution, and other corrupt activities. I

know motherhood is not ice cream because I am a young mother. Now, I can look back to appreciate and understand every hard lesson, all the support given to me, and every hug received from my mother. None of these things will ever be forgotten from such a phenomenal mother.

Yolanda Wellington

~ A BROKEN DREAM ~

Frances Wellington

What is a broken dream to you?

You don't even have a clue.

So how can you tell someone else what to do

about a missing piece to a once completed puzzle?

It's no way you can attempt to find

the missing puzzle piece that once was mine;

mine to hold onto forever, if I please,

mine to give away if I wish.

So don't tell me about a broken dream,

because this time you have no idea

how to describe how one might feel

one who has had a broken dream,

because I tell you they know the deal,

the deal about laughter, the deal about tears.

And if you had a broken dream,

you would know how it feels

to have broken heart,

and to also sit in the dark.

Out of the dark into the light,

My broken dream is ended now and that's a fact.

30 / NUGGETS FOR THE ROAD

A) Accept Christ into your life at an early age.

B) Mothers, make up your mind like I did and say like I did; *I will not lose my son to drugs or the streets.*

C) Mothers, tell your children, "I don't want you becoming a welfare recipient."

D) Fathers, spend time with your sons, teach them things. While hunting, my husband taught our son how to load and unload a gun.

E) Fathers, keep teaching. My husband taught my son the ins and outs of being an engineer.

F) Young people, you have to finish school to get a good job and not depend on others.

G) Fathers, your kids can always learn, even through fun things. My son's father taught him about racing cars while they were at the race track.

H) Let your kids see you working. My boy rode a yellow toy car while at work with his dad.

I) Young people, honor your father and mother that your days may be long on this earth. *Ex. 20:12*

J) Everyone, we are not quitters. If anyone tells you that you can't, ignore them and keep trying.

K) Keep moving, there is always an open door. Just believe in yourself.

L) Trust God for all or trust Him for nothing.

M) Mothers, say it like I did, and mean it when your kids act up. "I'm going hit you so hard you will see stars."

N) Tell them and mean this too. "I will knock you into next week."

O) Let everybody know, like I do; "I am not to be played with, but I am to be reckoned with."

P) Parents, say it and mean it when your kids act out. "I'm going to jack you up."

Q) "I will snatch a knot in you so big it will take three days to get it out."

R) Young people, wait until you get married to have sex, because it is against the bible. Doing so will save you a lot of heartache.

S) If you decide you can't wait, well I suggest you put on three rain coats. Use protection.

T) Everybody, money doesn't grow on trees. Save. Pay your bills. Have good credit.

U) Be responsible for your actions, there are always consequences.

V) Say like I say when it's time to get down to business, "It's on and cracking."

W) Keep people guessing; never let your right hand know what the left hand is doing.

X) For the haters, talk is cheap, but don't put your hands on me.

Y) Remind your kids that are determined to be rebellious that there are always consequences.

Z) Keep your dignity. Never stoop to anyone else's level.

A Bonus Nugget…

When I cut you, you are cut and it will take every cop on the east side of the Mississippi to find a bandage large enough to cover the gash. Meaning it's not a physical cut, but when I'm through with you, everybody will know it.

…Speaking of toxic friends, relationships, or anybody that needs to be cut off.

Persevere.

4-18-13

Richard

Thank You
for all I your
support. May God
forever bless you always

CPSIA information can be obtained at www.ICGtesting.com
Printed in the USA
LVOW010511100413

328478LV00006B/8/P